Retaining Expert
Knowledge

Retaining Expert Knowledge
What to Keep in an Age of Information Overload

Peggy Salvatore

CRC Press
Taylor & Francis Group
Boca Raton London New York

CRC Press is an imprint of the
Taylor & Francis Group, an **informa** business

AN AUERBACH BOOK

CRC Press
Taylor & Francis Group
6000 Broken Sound Parkway NW, Suite 300
Boca Raton, FL 33487-2742

First issued in paperback 2022

ISBN 13: 978-1-03-247620-9 (pbk)
ISBN 13: 978-1-138-29636-7 (hbk)
ISBN 13: 978-1-351-00290-5 (ebk)

DOI: 10.1201/9781351002905

Visit the eResources: https://www.crcpress.com/9781138296367

Library of Congress Cataloging-in-Publication Data

Names: Salvatore, Peggy, author.
Title: Retaining expert knowledge : what to keep in an age of information overload / Peggy Salvatore.
Description: Boca Raton : Taylor & Francis, 2017. | Includes bibliographical references and index.
Identifiers: LCCN 2018000798 (print) | LCCN 2018006056 (ebook) | ISBN 9781351002905 (e) | ISBN 9781138296367 (hardback : acid-free paper)
Subjects: LCSH: Knowledge management. | Specialists. | Employee retention.
Classification: LCC HD30.2 (ebook) | LCC HD30.2 .S255 2017 (print) | DDC 658.4/038--dc23
LC record available at https://lccn.loc.gov/2018000798

**Visit the Taylor & Francis Web site at
http://www.taylorandfrancis.com**

**and the CRC Press Web site at
http://www.crcpress.com**

Contents

PREFACE   xi

ACKNOWLEDGEMENTS   xv

AUTHOR   xix

PART I   THE OUTFLOW OF CORPORATE KNOWLEDGE

CHAPTER 1	THE LARGEST GENERATION LEAVES A GAP	3
	Out with the Old	4
	A Working with SMEs Methodology	5
	Shallow Learning: Learning, Learning Everywhere…	6
	The World's Oldest Profession	7
	Content Curation for Shallow Learning	9
	Content Curation for Deep Learning	9
	Push and Pull Learning	11
	The Wide and Wild World Web	11
	Learning How to Think Like an Expert	13
	Teaching Critical Thinking Skills	14
	Making Decisions and Judgment Calls about Value	16
	Deep Knowledge Knows Where Your Company Is Going	16
	More about Lost Organizational Knowledge	19
	Recycle and Curate	20
	Ongoing Evaluation and Review Cycles	21
	Continuous Process Improvement Knowledge Management Flowchart	23

CHAPTER 2   PRIORITIZE YOUR CORPORATE ASSETS   25
             Examine Your Organizational Chart   25
             Organizational Forgetting   28
             Have a Plan   28
             Capture Your Competitive Advantages   30
             Your Value and Distinction   30
             Knowledge Mapping   33
             How to Complete the Competitive Advantages Diagram   36
             The Value of the Exercise   37

CHAPTER 3   SUCCESSION PLANNING WITH YOUR SMEs   39
             Name Your Gurus   39
             About the Functional Area Exercise   40
             The Reluctant SME   42
             Your SME Catch and Release Program: The Process of
             Retirement and Rehirement   44
             Special Section: Succession Planning for Family-Owned
             Businesses   46
             The Engineering Whiz: A Founder's Succession Planning   47
             The Cement King: Wresting Control from the Heirs   47
             Less Happy Endings   48

CHAPTER 4   THE EXPERTS' DISCERNMENT   51
             Prioritize and Organize Your Assets   51
             Identifying Critical Assets: Your Value and Distinction   52
             Focus on Critical Information   53
             Knowledge Stratification   56
             Find Knowledge and Training Gaps   57
             Checklist: Find Your Knowledge and Training Gaps   57
             How to Prioritize the 4 Ms   58
                 Drill Down into Target Area Man   58
             Leadership and Influence Is throughout Your Company   59
             Prioritize and Organize Your Man Assets   60
             The Knowledge and Training Gap Exercise   60
             Find Your Gaps   61
             Drill Down into Target Area Machine   62
             Computers and More   62
             Prioritize and Organize Your Information   63
             The Knowledge and Training Gap Exercise   63
             Find Your Gaps   64
             Drill Down into Target Area Materials   65
             When a Common Material May Not Be So Common   66
             The Materials You Produce   66
             Prioritize and Organize Your Information   66
             The Knowledge and Training Gap Exercise   67
             Find Your Gaps   69
             Drill Down into Target Area Methods   69

Some Methods and Processes Can Be Easily Replicated 69
When a Method or Process Is Proprietary 69
Prioritize and Organize Your Information 70
The Knowledge and Training Gap Exercise 70
Find Your Gaps 71
Time and Resource Commitment 71

PART II KNOWLEDGE MANAGEMENT IN
THE AGE OF EXPONENTIAL
TECHNOLOGICAL ADVANCES

CHAPTER 5 COLLECTION, STORAGE, AND DELIVERY
CHALLENGES FOR CAPTURING EXPERTISE 77
Learning Transfer with the Multigenerational Workforce 79
Mutual Respect and Low Threat Interactions 80
Entitlement 80
For the Older Gen 80
For the Younger Gen 81
Young Workers Have the Greater Challenge 81
Dan Rockwell's 7 Ways Young Leaders
Succeed with Elders 82
Intergenerational Challenges Affect Learning Transfer 82
Technological Comfort Zone 83
Age-Related Illnesses and Biological Changes 86
Peaceful Coexistence 87

CHAPTER 6 CREATING A TECH PLAN FOR CAPTURING
EXPERTISE 89
Step One: Determine the Kind of Information You Are
Collecting 89
Step Two: Collect Knowledge in Formats
That Complement It 90
Step Three: Store and Translate the Information into
Learning Materials 92
What Kinds of Expertise Can You Capture? All Kinds! 93
About KSAs 94
About Knowledge 94
About Skills 95
About Attitudes 95

CHAPTER 7 THE BENEFITS OF TERRIFIC TECHNOLOGY 97
Before You Buy, Remember: Technology Changes 98
Learning Styles Change 99
Technology – The Story That AI Built 101
Technology – Ease of Use, Storage, and Transfer 101
Thinking Much Longer Term 104
Learning Librarian as Content Curator 106

CHAPTER 8 ASSESSING FUTURE LEARNING NEEDS IN AN
           AGE OF INDUSTRIAL DISLOCATION   107
           Peer around Corners into the Future   107
           What Business Are You Really In?   110
           Kodak as the Poster Child for #InnovationFail   111
           A Word about Historical Preservation   112

PART III   THE NATURE OF EXPERTISE AND
           THE ART OF MANAGING EXPERTS

CHAPTER 9 THE NATURE OF EXPERTISE   119
           A Real Methodology for Working with SMEs that
           Respects Everyone   120
           The Trouble with SMEs   120
           The Four Stages of Learning Model and Your SME   121
           Managing Experts   122

CHAPTER 10 KNOWLEDGE CAPTURE USING EXPERTS WITHIN
           THE PROVEN ADDIE FRAMEWORK   127
           Your Assigned SME and the ADDIE Process   129
           When to Use a Dedicated SME: Handholding   130
           Considerations for a *Working with SMEs* Methodology 132
           The Content Developer's Job When Working with Experts 133

CHAPTER 11 MANAGING THE 10 TYPES OF EXPERTS   137
           Encountering the Perfect SME   138
           The Speedy SME's Defining Characteristics   139
           The Creative, Scattered SME's Defining Characteristics 140
           The Shortcut SME's Defining Characteristics   142
           The Defensive SME's Defining Characteristics   144
           The Not-Quite-Expert SME's Defining Characteristics 145
           The Overcommitted SME's Defining Characteristics 147
           The Confounding SME's Defining Characteristics   149
           The SME Interrupted's Defining Characteristics   151
           Reckless Reviewer's Defining Characteristics   153
           The Reluctant SME's Defining Characteristics   155
           When All Else Fails: The Dedicated SME or SME for Hire 157

CHAPTER 12 TIPS, TOOLS, AND CHECKLISTS FOR
           WRANGLING EXPERTS   161
           Tips, Tricks, and Tools for Content Developers and Project
           Managers   162
           Tear Sheet #1: Project Plan Checklist   163
           Tear Sheet #2: Write a Project Charter   165
               Purpose of the Charter   165

About the Client 165
Project Overview 165
Project Goals 165
Expected Outcomes 165
Content 165
Audience 166
Deliverable Requirements 166
Assessment and Evaluation 166
Upfront Planning, Ongoing Project Management, and
Project Schedule 166
Assumptions 166
Project Alerts 167
Project Style Guidelines 167
Tear Sheet #3: Project Charter Checklist 168
Tear Sheet #4: Checklist for Gathering and Organizing
Information from Your Subject Matter Experts 172
Conduct a Well Planned Interview 172
Be a Project Manager 172
Create a Schedule and Plan 172
Tear Sheet #5: Common Sense Guidelines for Project
Managers 173
Tear Sheet #6: Roles and Responsibilities Chart 174
Tear Sheet #7: Subject Matter Expert Contact List 175
Tear Sheet #8: Content Gathering Session Cover Sheet 176
Content Gathering Session Cover Sheet 176
Tear Sheet #9: Standard Interview Questions 177
Tear Sheet #10: Expert Interview Checklist 178
Tear Sheet #11: Review Cycle Capture Log 179
Tear Sheet #12: SME Acknowledgement of Review 181
Tear Sheet #13: Follow-Up and Wrap-Up Signoffs 182
Tear Sheet #14: Project Evaluation Checklist 183
Tear Sheet #15: After Action Review Template 184
Tips, Tricks, and Tools for Subject Matter Experts 185
SME Tear Sheet #1: Process Tips for the Expert Content
Contributor 186
SME Tear Sheet #2: Top 10 Tips for Experts: How to
Provide Great Information 188

CHAPTER 13 EXPERTS OF THE FUTURE 191
Dueling Experts: When You Must Decide 191
A Societal Application: When Passions Are Inflamed,
Reason Flees 191
Managing Tomorrow's Experts: Are Traditional Experts
and NextGen Experts Different? 193
Will Artificial Intelligence Make Your Experts Extinct? 195
I Do Not Digress 199

Making a Plan to Retain Human Knowledge Until the
Robots Take Over   200

BIBLIOGRAPHY   201
INDEX   205

Preface

Retaining Expert Knowledge blends two self-published books and goes beyond them to explore the future of capturing and transferring expertise. The scope of the first book, *Working with SMEs: Gathering and Organizing Content from Subject Matter Experts,* simply established a methodology and best practices for interviewing subject matter experts to capture their knowledge for training programs. It assumed organizations knew exactly the critical knowledge they needed to capture and the people who were carrying around the most important information. However, a few questions arose from ensuing discussions about subject matter expertise that begged to be answered:

Are we talking to the right subject matter experts?

What knowledge should organizations capture?

What knowledge needs to be captured immediately as opposed to eventually?

If we have limited resources or limited time, which experts are most important to speak with first?

In light of these questions, it became clear the issue of identifying the right experts is entirely separate, and, in fact, as I spoke with people about the idea, I discovered it is actually a more critical problem. That led to the second book, *Finding Your SMEs: Capturing Knowledge from Retiring Subject Matter Experts Before They Leave.*

Here's why.

This decade, from 2010 to 2020, will see the largest recorded exit of talented and knowledgeable workers from your organizations as baby boomers head for sunny golf courses and extended vacations to enjoy the fruits of lifetimes of labor. In their wake, they leave their former employers understaffed and, even scarier, under-informed. In fact, I will go out on a limb here to suggest we are currently undergoing the largest transfer of knowledge in human history.

We are currently undergoing the largest transfer of knowledge in human history.

From the turn of the 20th to the turn of the 21st centuries, humankind experienced the greatest leaps in technological advances in recorded history. From horse-drawn buggies to space travel, human intelligence and creativity catapulted us from a plodding, linear existence to soaring, exponential possibilities. Books like Alvin Toffler's *Future Shock* first chronicled this geometric explosion of knowledge while Peter Diamandis' books, *Bold* and *Abundance,* took us the rest of the way toward the melding of humans and machines to remake the humanity that brought us here.

The purpose of this book is not to recount those books or to retread that ground. Rather, it is to recognize that the same human knowledge and creativity that got us here will get us there. So with the rapid acquisition of new knowledge – some estimates say knowledge now doubles every 2 years – it is important that we identify our journey and catalogue it individually and collectively.

The whole of human knowledge is a big bite for anybody, especially you and me operating in isolation. However, taken one person, one company, and one organization at a time, we can preserve what we have done so others can replicate it. To many practitioners at the organizational level, knowledge capture is a training function. But a full knowledge capture goes beyond the practical and immediate application of developing a training program for employees to continue the best practices. Each organization has a history, a culture, and knowledge that went before that may have lost its current relevance but not its importance. It is that broader vision of knowledge capture that this book addresses.

As we rapidly move toward artificial intelligence and computer generated activities that simulate human functions, it behooves us more than ever to preserve the knowledge, skills, and attitudes that makes us essentially human, if for no other reason than to create an accurate history.

Having defined the vision and the mission, this book is intended to provide readers with the ability to preserve their corporate knowledge with tools to assess your circumstance and judge the value of what you would labor and spend valuable resources to capture.

Yes, this is a training resource, but it also aspires to be a business resource. When knowledge is proliferating at the current rate and the culture is changing at a similar clip, it is a good time to step back and determine what has been important to your success, where you are today, and what it will take to stay in the game tomorrow.

For some companies, they may find that the buggy whips they made in 1860 bear no resemblance to the car parts they make today. And with the evolution of human transport, the car parts they make today may soon be obsolete. Perhaps that company will survive another incarnation or it will close its doors as new challenges do not resemble closely enough the old ones.

One study published in MIT Technology Review in September 2013 showed that the average company listed on the S&P 500 in 1958 had an average life on the exchange of 61 years. In comparison, a company today can expect to stay listed for a mere 18 years.[*] Companies become delisted as what they knew that spelled success yesterday is no longer relevant when tastes, needs, and technology change, and the pace of that trajectory is accelerating.

Your company houses knowledge, skills, attitudes, intellectual property, trade secrets, company culture, and individuals who will never be replicated exactly as they are today. Because they have demonstrated value in the past or are demonstrating value today, those treasures are worth preserving. Without a crystal ball, you cannot predict when or how you may need tomorrow what you know today.

So, whether you are looking to capture knowledge to train new employees, preserve company history or analyze what you have got

---

[*] Accessed September 1, 2017 at https://www.technologyreview.com/s/519226/technology-is-wiping-out-companies-faster-than-ever/.

today to build new products and services for tomorrow, your company is well-served by preserving the knowledge under your roof before it leaves.

After all, many of the retiring people under your roof today have had within their lifetimes relationships with people who were at the beginning of this unfolding rapid human evolution. My grandmother was born in 1896. When she drew her first breath, horse-drawn wagons delivered ice and milk to her kitchen doorstep. When she passed away in 2002, I was working from home on a computer that connected me instantaneously to customers around the world. It is unlikely that humans will ever be called on to preserve the large amount and disparate kinds of knowledge that we have acquired in the past 120 years.

Specifically, what has happened and is happening in your organization is part of this story. For now, and for the remainder of this book, let us focus on your company's role in its industry and the future.

Additional e-resource material is available from the CRC Press website: http://www.crcpress.com/9781138296367.

Acknowledgements

This book would not exist without Michael Militus of Computer Aid, Inc. whom I met through my interest in the Project Management Institute where he serves as Director of Programs for the Lehigh Valley region. Michael introduced me to the acquisition editor, John Wyzalek, at Taylor & Francis Group and work on this book began soon after. Thank you so much, Michael and John, for your interest in these ideas and the opportunity to develop them.

The original subject matter expert book came out of discussions with Jonena Relth, my good friend and owner of TBD Consulting and founder of MyCoreformance, Inc. Jonena and I talked about the idea for a subject matter expert book in our cross-country road trip from Bethlehem, Pennsylvania to Phoenix, Arizona via Route 66 dragging a U-Haul trailer behind her trusty SUV in 2014. She contributed substantial material to the first book, *Working with SMEs: A Guide to Gathering and Organizing Content from Subject Matter Experts.* Our MyCoreformance colleague, instructional designer, and project manager, Esther Groves, made important comments to the first version and editor, Heather Rodriquez, cleaned up the first pass. Amy Hanagan, CFO, and her husband and CEO, Luke, keep the whole MyCoreformance crew together and allow all of us to be creative and have fun. Jonena and the MyCore team have my eternal gratitude for all they have done for me and this work.

One of the early proponents of the first book, Michael Kolowich, founder of KnowledgeVision, Inc. and creator of software for experts, Knovio, has remained an advocate of this work, and I remain grateful. His first marketing director, Susan Zaney, teased me calling me "the SME's SME", and it stuck. Susan's successor, Marianne Rocco, has been very helpful in continuing to promote the subsequent books through webinars and blogs. Marianne inadvertently contributed to the title of this book when she asked me to create a webinar about how to wade through information overload. Knovio has been a friend of *Working with SMEs* and I am very thankful for their ongoing input and support.

The second subject matter expert book, *Finding Your SMEs: Capturing Knowledge from Retiring Subject Matter Experts in Your Organization Before They Leave,* is the bedrock upon which the concept for this book is built. For that, I have to thank several people whose discussions led me to want to answer the question, "Are we talking to the right experts?" Ken Petelinkar and John Lewis, co-founders of AGXPE, an association for best practices in the pharmaceutical industry, were interested in the working with experts' methodology; they invited me to present at the AGXPE inaugural annual meeting in Annapolis, Maryland in 2015 where I made some new friends and met future colleagues. In the workshop, I explored the question of whether we are talking to the right experts and collected some initial data to build a methodology. When I announced that I was developing that work, I got a call from trainer, Rick Kramer, at Carpenter Technologies, Inc. (while I was visiting the Rock and Roll Hall of Fame) asking when I would write the next book because the issue of retiring experts was high on everyone's list of problems. I developed the *Finding Your SMEs* workshop out of that conversation; we piloted it at CarTech where I learned more in that session that further informed the work. And that workshop became a book.

Some other people and organizations have knowingly or unknowingly made a positive difference in advancing this work. The C.F. Martin Company granted approval to be a case study. We love Martin Guitar here in the Lehigh Valley and are so proud to have them as part of the community. If you are ever in Nazareth, Pennsylvania, you must take the Martin tour where you can watch how guitars are made by hand. It is a thing of beauty. CEO of Synapse, Ryan Austin, contributed content to the technology section and has promoted the Working with SMEs methodology through blogs and promotion on his company website. Eric Blumthal, founder and owner of QMindshare, a microlearning tool, contributed content to the technology section. Professor Karl Kapp, author of several books on instructional technology, graciously invited me in the spring of 2017 to speak about this book in its earliest stages at Bloomsburg University and I thank him for the opportunity. I owe a debt of gratitude to friend and author of *Open Source Instructional Design*, Nathan Eckel, who introduced me to Karl Kapp and co-hosted a season of podcasts for the Working with SMEs website to advance the ideas in *Finding Your SMEs*.

Of course, this book would not be in your hands or in this fine condition but for the help of the people at Taylor & Francis Group, especially Stephanie Place-Retzlaff and Rebecca Dunn.

Others have been along on the journey this past year as business advisors and helping hands: James Lake for helping to develop the business model behind the workshops, Roland Thompson for business advice, authors Dallas and Nancy Demmitt of *Can You Hear Me Now?* for contributing a case study and a listening ear, Martin Gilligan for sharing his legal and business experience as well as a case study. I am grateful to an unsuspecting Jon Acuff, author of *Finish*, for his online Finish support program that gave me the organization and motivation to finish the manuscript on time as I checked off each day on the Finish calendar and added to the word count. Finally, as I have seen written in many other Acknowledgement sections and now appreciate more than ever, I am certain I have not mentioned nearly all the people who have contributed ideas, energy, and encouragement, and I apologize for any omissions.

Through it all, my dear friends, Stephen Bingham, Debbie Collins Pulcini, and Joe Pulcini are my trusted sounding boards. Their ideas, insights, support, and encouragement keep me going.

All good things start with the people on the home front. My son, Ben Heidorn, and daughters, Ellie and Molly Heidorn, provide me with more inspiration and encouragement than any mom could ever hope for or deserve. With the support of his wife, Rachel, Ben gives time and energy to my work, keeps my website humming along, and all four have kept the home fires burning while I toiled in the home office. I am truly blessed.

Author

Peggy Salvatore is a business writer, author, and training consultant working with organizations to help them preserve valuable corporate assets. She has a BA in journalism from Temple University and an MBA with a concentration in strategy and economics from New York Institute of Technology. In her early career, she worked as a full-time daily newspaper reporter covering government and politics culminating in covering a U.S. presidential campaign. She then began her own consultancy writing public policy, business, and economics articles mostly for the pharmaceutical industry. She also wrote training guides to educate physicians and pharmacists on the business of healthcare leading to her interest in corporate knowledge management. She has written or ghostwritten several business and personal biographies and is the author of numerous magazine and journal articles both in general business and healthcare. Recently, she assembled her experience in two self-published books on managing corporate knowledge. In January 2015, she published *Working with SMEs: A Guide to Gathering and Organizing Content for Subject Matter Experts*. In November 2016, she released *Finding Your SMEs: Capturing Knowledge from Retiring*

Subject Matter Experts in Your Organization Before They Leave. Through her weekly blogs and ongoing client contact, this work continues to expand. Peggy speaks and presents workshops on how to work with subject matter experts to preserve corporate expertise for business continuity. Her work can be found at www.workingwithsmes.com.

PART I

THE OUTFLOW OF CORPORATE KNOWLEDGE

1

THE LARGEST GENERATION
LEAVES A GAP

Your organization grew and prospered under the direction of several large generations of educated and driven individuals. First, the World War II generation, also called The Greatest Generation, has almost completely left the workforce taking with it a unique set of attitudes and behaviors that allowed corporations to thrive in a linear way. Next, their children, Baby Boomers, who became if not the greatest, then certainly The Largest Generation, carried many of their parents' ideals to work with them.

The Boomers, however, have a few unique characteristics that evolved corporate values and structures to be more responsive to individuals. Boomers' values begat an agile and mission-driven workforce as opposed to the formal organizational structure of the World War II generation.

While this book is not a social or labor history of the post-World War II corporate workforce, suffice it to say that a very large, educated, and dedicated labor cohort is exiting the workforce taking with them values, knowledge, and experience that, in many cases, may be the secret to your organization's success. It is within their historical context that we can understand what they are taking with them.

In fact, the workforce has entered a unique period between 2015 and 2020 when fully five generations will be in the labor pool at the same time. As recent Bureau of Labor Statistics data shows, people over 65 are staying in the workforce longer for many reasons, but mostly for economic ones. While they are sticking around and imparting wisdom, the younger wait to truly seize the reins. Some signs indicate they are no longer waiting and are upending old traditions and structures. In this tension, the value of decades of valuable information may be caught in the undercurrents of resentment, ambition, and impatience to get on with the future.

Out with the Old

Organizational development experts have given much attention to the interpersonal challenges of this circumstance. You can hire any number of experts who will train you how to work to successfully integrate the styles of multiple generations in the workforce. Let me suggest the tensions extend beyond the social implications of this phenomenon. This particular demographic distribution, as seen in Figure 1.1, demonstrates a convergence of talents, skills, and attributes that need to be conveyed not from one generation to the next but perhaps from one generation to another that is three degrees removed from it. That transfer presents several challenges including both what and how that learning is relayed. It is also happening in a time of technological advances that alter assumptions about what is important.

Generational filters require that knowledge, skills, and attitudes (KSAs in training parlance) not only be captured, but also preserved and translated in such a way that the knowledge itself

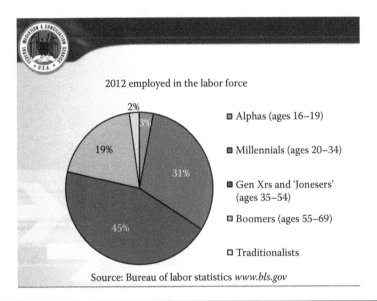

Figure 1.1   Five generations in the workplace*

---

* Accessed on September 15, 2017 at https://malmc.org/documents/2014Presentations/ 5Generations-1Workplace-LuAnnGlaser.pdf. Slide 19.

remains relevant and usable to a workforce with different frames of reference.

It is in this context that we will explore the challenge of finding your experts and preserving their knowledge in ways that make it accessible to their grandchildren and great-grandchildren.

A Working with SMEs Methodology

A Working with SMEs methodology creates a system for identifying and transferring the critical knowledge and talent of your subject matter experts that is leaving the workforce in unprecedented numbers given this unique confluence of circumstances. In order to understand the situation, it helps to reflect on the context of the kind of labor that is leaving your organization. In that spirit, each business must examine the kinds of knowledge, skills, and attitudes (KSAs) that undergird your successful organization so that you can accurately identify what to capture and how to capture it.

When people leave, the worst thing that can happen is that they take critical skill sets with them that you cannot replace. The second worst thing that can happen is that, when you discover they possessed irreplaceable pieces of your corporate puzzle, you hire them back as consultants at exorbitant rates on their own time schedules. The best outcome is that you use their last, best years with your company capturing what they know. If you are shooting for the best outcome, the Working with SMEs methodology is a process for memorializing their successes.

Meanwhile, you can feel an almost perceptible anxiety around the imminent retirement of the Baby Boomer generation. In casual and formal discussions on workforce training, leaders in business and industry worry openly about what will happen in the next 5–10 years when a huge bulk of talent walks out the doors of the local businesses that count on them. The Working with SMEs methodology is designed to give you a system for catching that important information before it leaves and provides your business with a knowledge management plan to preserve and transfer it to new generations of employees.

In these next chapters, we will delve into the questions to help you determine the *how, what, why,* and *where* to capture critical knowledge.

One question, though, is easy to answer. You need read no further to find out *when* to capture your critical organizational knowledge. The answer is Now.

Shallow Learning: Learning, Learning Everywhere...

With some reluctance, I use the words "shallow learning." But, in truth, the rapid pace of change and technological advances have made much learning a quick-hit endeavor. We live in a world of constant growth and innovation on a global level, and that has begotten a generation of shallow learners. Shallow learning is not necessarily a bad thing, and it is quite necessary to keep pace with new information.

But collecting information, developing training, and storing and transferring knowledge for shallow learners is much different than it is for deep learners. Shallow learning actually is most appropriate for many jobs. Shallow learning assumes you only need to know what you need to do to accomplish the task at hand. That task may be on an assembly line doing a repetitive task, or it may be in a service job repeating specific functions and interactions according to a predetermined script or set of actions. Repetition in most jobs is a good thing because it means a job is being achieved within certain guidelines or best practices guaranteeing defined quality and outcomes.

While shallow learning works for many jobs and most tasks – or snippets of jobs – many other jobs require deep learning. When a job requires deep learning, usually the worker is hired with a strong skill set and knowledge base. It is your company's job to customize your internal deep knowledge assets for these workers so they can acquire your organization's specific knowledge and goals. You hire the right knowledge and skill set to accomplish the tasks and then manage your human assets in a way that you can take advantage of their experience and education to achieve your corporate purpose. When you have a full grasp of the abilities of your knowledge workers, you can assemble and disseminate the correct corporate knowledge to them to accomplish your goals.

Knowledge acquisition is a two-way street as well. Your deep knowledge workers will contribute to your corporate body of knowledge to make it relevant to changes in the marketplace and industry. Deep knowledge workers by definition have a 360° view of their subject that most of your workforce does not share.

Because your deep knowledge workers come to you with a skill set and experience behind them, they also enter your organization with a lot of preconceived ideas about how things should work. After all, certain ways of doing things have worked for them before. The danger of bringing in high value knowledge workers is that they may shape your organization in ways that you did not intend and that do not serve your long-term vision for your business. For this reason, your deep knowledge workers need to be involved in the strategic initiatives and direction of your goals for the organization so the horsepower that you engaged when you hired them is pulling in the same direction as leadership intends.

We will talk more about strategic planning in the second part of the book, but for now tuck away in the back of your mind that everything we discuss between here and there assumes alignment with a vision that is well-conceived and faithfully executed. How you achieve that strategic plan – and how you engage your experts and leaders in designing it – is discussed later.

The World's Oldest Profession

The world's oldest profession is not what you think! Training is actually the world's oldest profession. When the first human babies popped out of the first human mamas, the mamas immediately ramped up knowledge, skills, and attitudes transfer. I was not there and have not actually seen this documented, but it is a fairly safe bet. If mama did not transfer her acquired wisdom to her child, the species would not have survived. And therein lies the foundation for my assumption.

> You can eat this; it is safe.
> Stay away from that animal; it is dangerous.
> Put one foot in front of the other like this.
> Do not forget to put your napkin in your lap and start with the silverware on the outside of your place setting.

Mamas have been keeping babies safe and viable in their environments by imparting acquired wisdom from the beginning of time. So I rest my case. Training is the world's oldest profession.

Extending this example, critical, just-in-time information is the heart of learning and doing.

Early childhood learning is all about see one and do one – *Tie your shoes by bringing this loop around.*

Early childhood learning is about immediate feedback – *I told you not to touch the stove!*

Early childhood learning is about mentoring – *Next time she teases you, tell her how that makes you feel.*

Early childhood learning relies on these strategies in the moment because they work. Those same methods have served industrial and business knowledge, skills, and attitudes transfer since we hammered out the second wheel. Again, I wasn't there, but it is a safe assumption that the human who smoothed out the rough edges on the first wheel figured out a plan for replicating the process and told the next person. And that approach became the way it was done.

Early childhood education from mother to child is about the value of short, demonstrative, and immediate learning opportunities.

In the fashion of the watchful caregiver, the uptake of just-in-time educational videos and smartphone reminders allows employees to have tutors and mentors at their fingertips all day long. The training industry is learning how to take advantage of this development in on-demand learning. Short video and electronic smartphone snippets of on-the-job training and reminders are sophisticated extensions of the old-fashioned paper job aid posted in a workstation.

These electronic job aids provide heretofore impossible access to experts. No matter what your experts do for you, whether she is the best assembler on the floor or he is the best accountant in your department, make sure they are documenting their actions using short, transferable snippets because all the pieces of their aggregated wisdom becomes the bedrock of knowledge transfer.

You can build larger and more intensive learnings from these pieces, but it is important to collect these learning components *in situ.*

We will discuss how you collect information, how you choose what to collect, and how to bottle it for consumption later. For now, the immediate important fact is that humans learn best in the moment, when they need it. So capturing and preserving information from experts to be accessed on an as-needed basis is the foundation of knowledge transfer for your organization.

With all this valuable expertise floating around, leaders need to identify it and employees need guidance to find it after it has been captured.

Content Curation for Shallow Learning

Content curation for shallow learning jobs is a matter of gathering or making available short snippets of information so they are easy to understand and storing them in a way that they can be easily retrieved when needed.

For example, let us say your new line workers need to recall the exact order for attaching the colored wires to the doodad. They may have a step-by-step job aid at their workstation to help them get it straight. But sometimes the tricky attachment method is slowing down their inexperienced hands. That is when it is time to fire up the tablet and watch the demonstration again. A well-curated training platform will give the worker at that station quick access to the tasks relevant to their role.

Just-in-time access to an expert demonstration achieves two things: (1) It gives the workers the information in the moment they need it – no waiting! (2) It frees the more experienced workers to continue working at their own stations, and at their own paces, without the constant interruptions of their apprentices.

While this is just one simple example, it demonstrates how just-in-time information is valuable when it is accessible immediately at the point of need.

When your knowledge management plan takes a 360°, 30,000-foot level view of the role of short, instructive content, it can assume its rightful place in a much larger plan for transfer of expertise down through time.

Content Curation for Deep Learning

At that full, high-level view, you can also see where the same kind of brief instructive content fits into your more intensive trainings.

Content curation for deep learners requires that the training function in your organization have a grasp of the specialized fields that are essential to your company's success, and how to engage workers in the constant evolution of knowledge. For deep knowledge workers, you may invest far more time in long-form training. But that doesn't mean short and sweet instruction is not useful as an adjunct.

One of the great challenges of knowledge transfer is how little of it sticks. The reason is often that too much information is given, much of it in a classroom out of the context of its use, so it becomes irrelevant data.

The best use of classroom, then, is to present the big ideas, generate discussion around them, and encourage initial interaction with the subject matter. Beyond that, learners remember what they need to know. When they return to the workplace, what better way to extend the learning and to reinforce newly introduced concepts than to make sure learners have the information available in snippets, demonstrations, and reminders where and when they are most likely to use it. Learning is best applied with employees where they meet the products and the customers.

After all, to paraphrase Ronald Reagan, so much of what we know is not true. Follow-up learning, repetition, and reinforcement is all about making sure what you think you remember is accurate and true.

Content curation for deep learning is about reinforcing concepts after the initial training and making the right information available to the right workers at the point of need.

Managing a menu of content to support deep knowledge workers is more complex than assembling a series of short instructions for a finite task, but the elements are the same.

Both shallow and deep learning just-in-time require a good knowledge framework and the ability to access what you need when you have a question or need clarification.

Providing just-in-time information requires both push and pull approaches. After all, sometimes workers will seek an answer on the job at random, but sometimes experts can anticipate their need and make sure that knowledge is available at that particular time and place. Knowing how and when knowledge is used is part of their expertise, so make sure your experts are involved in your content curation plan. They can help you put your learning segments in context for your employees.

Push and Pull Learning

Both shallow and deep learning are on push and pull bases. The content curator can account for both by assembling a well-indexed and easily accessible library of assets.

For push learning, managers and the training department can create learning pathways for individuals to enhance their performance. Push learning includes things like task checklists and established protocols for shallow learning and executive leadership training tracks for deep learning. Push learning is usually organized by the training function and pushed *out* to the learner at the point and time of need. Learners get a recommended – or most often required – pathway to acquire the KSAs required to perform their function to the satisfaction of their employers.

For pull learning, the training department's role is to anticipate the kinds of information that workers will seek spontaneously in the course of the execution of their roles. Pull learning is harder to curate because of the guesswork involved in the kind of information workers might need. However, the importance of cataloguing and providing pathways and guidance cannot be emphasized strongly enough because the point of curating pull content is to steer learners to appropriate material. As Catherine Lombardozzi, the author of *Learning Environments by Design*,* points out, one of the main goals of content curation is to make sure that learners are identifying the correct knowledge they seek from a wide and random world of information available on the Internet using a search engine. Part of the importance of anticipating questions and creating pathways is to make sure your workers are not learning how to do something according to the first hit on their Internet search, but rather finding information that is prescribed by company methods and best practices.

The Wide and Wild World Web

The Internet is a learner's best friend and a corporation's nightmare.
Why?
You can learn almost anything by putting terms in a search engine and exploring hundreds of pages of hits. The challenge for employees, trainers, and others interested in knowledge transfer in your

---

* *Learning Environments by Design*. Catherine Lombardozzi. ATD Press. 2016.

organization is to balance taking advantage of the Internet's nearly endless repository of information versus funneling seekers to a productive search result without wasting precious company resources on a proverbial wild goose chase.

Conversely, some companies have strict security policies that restrict web access; that limits the ability of employees to see anything other than approved content. Restricted access is often required for certain types of work or roles, and it can be appropriate. Restricted access can protect customers (e.g., patients in a health care setting) and information related to vendors and employees. It also creates an environment where the flow of information can be controlled to promote best practices within the walls of an organization.

A well-curated library of preapproved corporate resources can prevent fruitless or misdirected searches by your employees searching for information.

STORYTIME

I worked in a company where research was an essential part of my job. I spent hours researching diseases and therapeutic interventions. The world of biomedical research is vast and complex. We had a few primary filters: (1) the validity of the source (e.g., peer-reviewed journals or credible medical websites) and (2) timeliness (e.g., something from 2016 ranked before something published in 2010.) If you have spent any time doing research in complex sciences, you know that not only do the fields grow geometrically each year but also that scientific disciplines have different schools of thought. And then there is the filter of "lies, damn lies, and statistics," which allows even seasoned PhDs to respectfully disagree in their area of expertise. When you are working in a field that allows you to dabble in complex areas like Alzheimer's Disease, novices with such broad filters are using blunt instruments in a very fine working environment. The availability of information on the Internet is both a blessing and curse in these kinds of environments where generalists are making decisions about information in which even experts disagree. Having done research in the pre-Internet era, certainly it was a bit easier when knowledgeable colleagues sifted through data and sent me the relevant information according to their preferences. In the era of Internet research, the uninitiated can suffer from overexposure to only slightly relevant information that perplexes the research process. Expert guidance from content curators using an organization's filtering process is helpful in these situations.

Learning How to Think Like an Expert

...more than knowing a myriad of facts, expertise is a deep knowledge of the problems that continually arise on a particular job. It is accumulated over years of experience and is organized in the expert's mind in a way that allows him or her to overcome the limits of reasoning.

From The Experts in Your Midst *by Michael J. Prietula and Herbert A. Simon, Harvard Business Review, January–February 1989*

Yes, Virginia, you can teach employees how to think like an expert – or at least how to think in an organized way about the certain and specific things you would like them to think about.

Most deeply organized knowledge has some sort of methodology or tautology behind it, and that framework can and should be shared with learners. Due to the nature of expertise, perhaps your experts cannot clearly articulate how they arrive at their conclusions or make decisions related to their areas of expertise, but it is worth exploring this concept with them in an effort to have them share their mental processes. Usually with good prompting during a dedicated interview with your experts, you will learn the kinds of decisions they make and the conscious or unconscious decision trees they use to make them.

Many jobs require deep knowledge. Deep knowledge requires teaching thinking skills. Work with your subject matter experts to unearth the kinds of frameworks, methodologies, decision trees, resources, and analytic tools they use when they are confounded by a problem. As you take the time to try to understand their thinking processes, you will learn valuable information to pass on to other learners.

Deep knowledge can be harder to capture and more difficult to curate because you are not transferring small, digestible bits of information. Shallow knowledge is a one-bite *hors d'oeuvres*. Deep knowledge is a seven course meal. As such, present deep knowledge in the correct order and with the right implements for consumption.

When you approach capturing deep knowledge from your experts, you will probably need to stay focused on the benefits of teaching organized thinking to your learners. Remember, you are concerned with long-term results for your company by preserving and transferring these *critical thinking systems*. Basically, I am saying that you are unlikely to capture or preserve this kind of deep knowledge in one sitting with your experts. It can be a longer process for all of you and it takes patience. However, if you manage to unearth and bottle your experts' thinking patterns, your time and energy is well spent.

This kind of knowledge must be captured; its methods for capture are in Part III. For now, tuck away in the back of your mind that these considerations are essential to your knowledge management planning.

Teaching Critical Thinking Skills

Critical thinking is a type of expertise; one that you can teach and grow quickly within your organization. One of the greatest values that a true critical thinker can bring to the organization is the ability to look without fear or favor at all parts of your business. That requires turning a bright light on a series of questions that will illuminate where you are and where your business is headed.

Part of teaching expertise is to present the foundational principles behind the subject matter by imparting critical thinking skills that give learners the scaffolding they need to continue to learn.

Critical thinking skills are important...especially for people who are in leadership and decision-making positions. Big picture thinking about your business and your industry is an important part of knowledge management at the top, but it is also needed at all levels of the organization. Often, it is the people who are closest to the work who are most concerned about capturing what they know for business continuity, and they benefit from training in critical thinking skills to help them categorize what they know.

Your big picture thinking about your business and industry needs to include a well-thought-out knowledge management plan, or more specifically, the expertise you need to bottle and preserve to keep your organization running.

When it comes to your knowledge management plan, you need people trained in critical thinking skills to provide you with unblinking honesty about the state of your business and industry so you can steer it into the future with clear vision. Not everything that got you here will get you there. The future is moving faster than the average long-term plan, which is why long-term planning has fallen out of favor to agile product development and rapid prototyping. In this fail fast/fail forward business environment, your competitors have something coming off the proverbial drawing boards every day that can send your product development in another direction or send your existing product off the market completely.

An article in SmartBrief, *Learn the Art of Avoiding Action for the Sake of Action**, highlighted the difference between strategic planning and strategic thinking. Author Adriano Pianesi states, "Perhaps we're 'in the know' enough to recognize that many consider the discipline of strategic planning to have long gone the way of the dinosaurs."

Instead, Pianesi advocates strategic thinking as a response to the VUCA (volatile, uncertain, complex, and ambiguous) world in which we conduct business and live. It is a world that requires a bias toward action, *informed action*, but action nonetheless. Let me suggest it is informed action that still requires the type of long view thinking more characteristic of strategic planning than agile rapid response iteration. Rapid iteration is valuable in a *context that is driven from a deep understanding and analysis* of the factors driving your business, your industry, and the larger environment that is more characteristic of strategic planning.

Critical thinking skills among leaders produce good decisions made within a framework that makes sense based on everything you know and takes into consideration all the things you don't know. The challenge is that the list of things you do not know grows longer every day, and it makes critical thinking skills even more, well, critical.

---

* Accessed July 15, 2017 at http://www.smartbrief.com/original/2017/06/learn-art-avoiding-action-sake-action-0?utm_source=brief.

Making Decisions and Judgment Calls about Value

> The greatest single instrument of change is the advancement of the mathematical tools called algorithms and their related sophisticated software (machine learning, so-called soft AI, prediction engines and the like).
>
> Any organization that is not a math house now or is unable to become one soon is already a legacy company.
>
> *From* The Attacker's Advantage *by Ram Charan*

A natural analogue to critical thinking skills is the proliferation of big data. The knowledge housed in your organization is the companion to your company's greatest asset, your people. The right analysts ask the questions and interpret your data to mine your valuable assets in a structured way.

The important information you need to understand your company's advantages lies in your data. Your experts may be the employees who input data or analyze data. Or your experts may not be working directly with data at all; rather, their work generates data. In any case, if the answers to your company's questions lie in the data, it follows that anything important can be reconstructed by accessing the accumulated information stored in your information systems.

If your subject matter experts cannot specifically tell you what they know or how they intuitively figure things out, it is quite possible their knowledge can be reconstructed or reverse engineered from your intelligent systems. The advantage of working with your subject matter experts is that you may be able to circumvent what could be a lengthy and costly data analytic process if they can tell you what they know, how they know it, and where you can find it.

Deep Knowledge Knows Where Your Company Is Going

It bears repeating that much of the important information you need to preserve for business continuity is learning of the deeper kind. Some of your projections about the future of your company will come from intuition, some will come from running the filters and diagnostics in the charts presented in this book, and let me suggest that some of your answers about your company's direction require a deep dive into your data.

As you look toward the future, look clearly and closely at what you already know. Your data will tell you what has worked in the past, what is working today, what is changing, and what is no longer working. Pay attention to the numbers. Numbers do not lie despite my favorite saying, "There are lies, damn lies and statistics." The lies and damn lies derive from manipulating data to get a tainted result. Do not do that. You might think you are doing yourself, your board of directors, or your direct boss a favor by slicing and dicing data to present a more favorable picture than the one the numbers suggest. It will catch up with you. If your employees are underperforming, your customers are not paying their bills, your sales team is not bringing in revenue, or the public's buying patterns have changed, eventually those things will catch up with you and your ability to survive. Better to know sooner rather than later.

As you look clear-eyed at the story your data tells you about your company's performance and trajectory, that information can help you make decisions about what internal expertise is worth spending resources to preserve. If a certain product line is becoming obsolete, face it. Derive as much revenue from the product as you can today, but realize your future is elsewhere and preserve *that*.

Your corporate deep knowledge resides in your expertise. Let me suggest that part of your corporate expertise is your analyst's ability to interpret your business data and feed you correct projections. Your internal data is priceless in many ways, but for the purposes of this chapter, it is important in these two ways that I would like you to take away from this discussion:

1. The data will let you know what products and services are the future of your organization and where to spend your finite, valuable resources to preserve KSAs that support them.

2. The data analyst possesses deep knowledge of your business and, as such, should be among your valuable internal experts who possess critical knowledge relative to your competitive advantages. Make sure you are working with your data analysts and preserving *their* corporate expertise!

Working from the continuous quality improvement premise that you are always working in beta, yesterday's training, or knowledge assets may be outdated in one of several ways:

- The training method (length, technique)
- The information itself
- The transfer method (live classroom, e-learning, webinar, book, video, paper templates, etc.)
- The storage technology (or lack thereof)

With some reconsideration of what you already have, you can prevent the training you have already built with your valuable experts from becoming useless due to poor planning and execution. One of the ways to help your knowledge assets live through several technical and technique evolutions is to think through your platform choices as you transform your internal expertise into materials with usable and lasting value.

Review your capture method options and choose those that you believe from your vantage point will withstand the test of time. Knowledge captured on 5 1/4-inch floppy disks is in danger of being relegated to the trash bin of history. I know this from several firsthand experiences.

I wrote some leadership, time and project management training that was widely used as part of a business acumen series for a national drugstore chain. More than a decade later, I wanted to go back and review the content and update some of the concepts to repurpose it. The original training company vendor was acquired by a multinational and its old records are gone. And my original work is on...you guessed it...5 1/4 inch floppies that are useless in my new computer and laptop. Yes, it can be recaptured and transferred but at some aggravation and cost. Lesson learned.

In another instance, I wrote and recorded music on analog studio grade recording tape which was transferred to cassette. Those cassettes are degrading and, only recently, we were talking about moving those to digital formats. It is increasingly difficult to find – and increasingly expensive to hire – analog studios that have access to equipment to remix the original 3-inch mastering magnetic tapes, while the existing cassettes' quality are degenerating.

Bitter lessons learned, so take heed.

Today's latest technology seems like it will last forever, or at least long enough that you cannot imagine a time when you cannot access your knowledge assets. However, let me harken back to the original premise: We are living in a time of unprecedented change. Today's assumptions are tomorrow's miscalculations in retrospect. Nobody can be expected to have a crystal ball about the way we will store, retrieve, and transmit data in the next decade. You can only be certain it will not be the way we do it today.

Today's assumptions are tomorrow's miscalculations in retrospect.

This might seem a bit archaic, but in retrospect, one of the best ways to have preserved the original leadership training program would have been to print out pdfs on a good grade of paper using high- quality ink. Similarly, the slapdash method of writing and recording pop music bypasses the good, old formal method of written notation common to composing. We can still faithfully reproduce Beethoven because he wrote it down in a way that a learned musician can read and replicate it as intended. As magnetic tape recordings degrade, so does the original intent. As long as people are reading and writing in a commonly accepted lexicon, paper has longevity that electronic forms of reproduction lack.

More about Lost Organizational Knowledge

Shelfware goes nowhere and helps no one.

What is shelfware? Lots of corporate training departments have it. Shelfware is the name for those programs that companies spent hundreds of thousands, maybe millions, of dollars or euros or yuan to build only to sit there forgotten and eventually outdated.

Some shelfware is unavoidable. You may have built a training program anticipating regulations that got torpedoed by a government agency. It happens. I have seen it, done it, and seen customers pay for it. But just about every program you have developed has some inherent value. Something can be saved from it. The content might serve as background information or provide context for other uses; your outdated training programs probably contain great design ideas and activities that you can use somewhere else.

As an example, we built sales training for a pharmaceutical product that was rejected by the FDA. Ouch! The company spent millions building training programs about the disease state the new molecule was intended to address, about the new molecule itself, and about the competitive landscape. It often happens that a molecule is effective in other disease states and can be approved for those later. Some of the work we did could be repurposed later if or when the molecule is approved for some different condition. Some of that work may be able to be resurrected for related use.

That said, before you build anything new, see what you have in the attic. If you have spent time and money creating training programs, you most assuredly have something of value in them.

Recycle and Curate

Do not expect to save money by being able to avoid building unnecessary training programs. Sometimes you will build unnecessary training programs. Oh, well.

It is difficult to project how a market can change, leadership can redirect the enterprise, or regulations can expire – all things that happen all the time that can immediately make obsolete your well-conceived and well-designed knowledge management plan. You can often recycle some information assets and extract future value. This is extremely important as you consider how you will capture, preserve, and pass on expertise. Because people learn in snippets and expertise today may be outdated folklore tomorrow, it may not even be wise to spend an extraordinary amount of money on an elaborate training program anymore.

The way to maximize your training dollars is to spend your money differently so you are building agile programs in a flexible framework. Training dollars can be used to prioritize projects by urgency, to catalogue knowledge for future use, and to develop guidelines for content curation. When you put plans in place that anticipate change, you can pivot when the environment and your learners require it.

Technology demands that content curation is a necessary component of a training department. The fact that learners are now in 24/7 knowledge acquisition mode, and content is on demand means that the steady flow of information going into the heads of your employees needs to be sorted for relevance to their specific jobs. Relevance also needs to take into consideration their needs at this point in their careers and the lifecycle of the company. The roles of trainers and managers now include this important function of content curation to manage knowledge assets through these filters.

For a good discussion and overview of this important topic, I again refer you to Lombardozzi's book, *Learning Environments by Design*. I had the privilege of reading an early draft and participating in discussions with the author, and she was one of the leading edge thinkers in the training and talent development world to identify this issue as one that will drive corporate learning now and in the future.

Ongoing Evaluation and Review Cycles

Anticipating the organization and relevance of information is an essential component of modern knowledge management as is constant evaluation, updating, and circulation of that information. According to Ray Kurzweil's law of accelerating returns, knowledge now doubles every 12 months[*], which means you can expect that this constant state of progress affects your organizational knowledge map too.

After you have spent valuable, finite, corporate resources to find and capture critical information, it needs to be continually accessed, evaluated, and circulated to the people who need it. The people who evaluate your learning are an essential loop in the quality control chain, as your in-house experts review content for immediacy, relevancy, and accuracy. Due to the law of accelerating returns, you will frame your knowledge mapping process within a forward-looking strategic plan that takes into consideration the effect that technological changes will have on your industry, products, and the larger economic environment.

When you have a good continuous improvement plan in place, you are more likely to avoid shelfware by developing and using a good storage and retrieval system for your knowledge management programs to support them on the back end. While you may not be able to automate review cycles for all your internal knowledge components, you should be able to at least schedule review cycles for categories of knowledge that you have a reasonable expectation could become stale or expire. You know best the kind of information you are housing, so those judgment calls can only be made by the people in your organization with the bird's eye view.

---

[*] Accessed September 2, 2017 at http://www.kurzweilai.net/the-law-of-accelerating-returns.

Each company faces its own very unique challenges in assessing what knowledge currently exists in-house, what is relevant, and where it is kept. For some large, global corporations with many business units, it is more likely you will find massive duplication as layers of successive planners rebuilt the proverbial wheel. The challenge in these cases is to sort through what you have, evaluate it, and decide what still has value, can be updated, and retained.

On the other end of the spectrum are very small companies or companies for whom institutional knowledge resides in a few founders or legacy employees where the experts are taken for granted in the daily flow of business. In those cases, the challenge is usually that there is a dearth of codified information. Small, closely-held companies will find most useful the exercises on identification and collection of information from a few irreplaceable legacy employees, rather than the exercises that emphasize stratification, relevance, and finding gaps in a plethora of information scattered throughout the enterprise.

STORYTIME

Dallas and Nancy Demmitt run a counseling consultancy based on their book about listening skills, *Can You Hear Me Now?* While their business was built on a counseling practice, their method reached beyond individual clients and eventually they were brought in by a major national fast food chain to teach their principles to the corporate leadership. The Demmitts developed a full corporate program for one client that has application for others. As the Demmitts begin their eighth decade of life, they want to capture and codify the work they have done for two reasons: (1) They want to be able to put a process in place for their existing corporate customer to continue to benefit from the program. (2) They want to educate "multipliers" who can spread the listening skills process they have developed to improve corporate communications in other organizations as well as save marriages and improve individual lives.

The Demmitts' business is a case where the experts are already identified. The challenge is to decide how to capture, organize, and transfer their message so it can be delivered beyond themselves. That requires a close examination of the core competencies they possess, how they do what they do to make themselves valuable and inimitable to their client base, and a full examination of their business including the people, methods, processes, equipment, and materials used to deliver these services today.

I encourage companies to assess the knowledge they have already spent time and money to develop before spending more time and money developing more training programs. I would not say it here if I had not seen companies overlook valuable assets now collecting dust as shelfware while plowing new resources into duplicate materials. As you review existing knowledge assets, this may also be a time to gore some sacred cows – and consultants – in the interest of progress and savings. If you know what I am saying in that last sentence, this means you.

Continuous Process Improvement Knowledge Management Flowchart

As you think about capturing precious internal critical expertise for future use, and avoiding as much as humanly possible capturing knowledge that will be useless later, you will be employing a 360° view of your business. You are scanning your past for successes you want to preserve, you are looking into the future to predict what you need going forward to take advantage of new opportunities, and you are doing it in a framework that allows you to capture, preserve, and transfer corporate knowledge safely from employees you hired in 1960 to employees you will hire in 2060.

The following flowchart gives you a framework that expresses the ever-evolving process that is the knowledge management component of your business continuity plan. We will revisit this chart later, but for now, it is here to examine the elements of an ongoing evaluation of your knowledge map and to reinforce the idea that this process is iterative. You will revisit your decisions in the future, make new ones, and change your tactics to align with evolving strategy. Figure 1.2 demonstrates that all parts of the cycle are always in play somewhere in your organization. Knowledge management is an ongoing, living process.

Continuous Process Improvement Knowledge Management

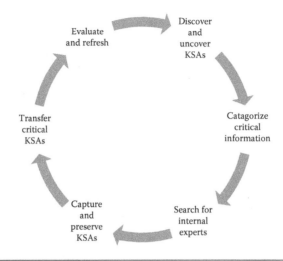

Figure 1.2   Continuous process improvement knowledge management flow cycle

1. Discover and uncover KSAs. Complete the competitive advantages diagram process and drill down to identify the knowledge, skills and, attitudes that make your company unique.
2. Categorize critical information. Distinguish among critical, essential, and non-essential information. Identify critical KSAs for business continuity.
3. Search for internal experts. Find your internal experts who are the keys to your success.
4. Capture and preserve KSAs. Work with your internal experts to capture your critical knowledge, skills, and attitudes in a way that authentically captures them and preserves them in a way that they can be transferred and replicated later.
5. Transfer critical KSAs. Choose the best methods for transferring knowledge, skills, and attitudes to others, especially focusing on an ADDIE framework to develop training using technology that will be available and usable in the future.
6. Evaluate and refresh. Review your current critical KSAs against the backdrop of your long-term strategic plan considering the rapid pace of change. As you identify new critical KSAs, repeat this process to capture, preserve, and transfer updated assets with the aid of your internal experts.

2

PRIORITIZE YOUR
CORPORATE ASSETS

When you are deciding what information you need to capture for future leaders and employees, ask yourself, "What is the distinction and value that our company brings to our customers?" Make sure you know what goes into the secret sauce in your company's Funburger so you can preserve those elements of your winning game.

Think about these kinds of issues:

- What is/are your company's core competency or competencies?
- What are your competitive advantages?
- *Who* is a competitive advantage? Do you have a particularly charismatic or public leader? Do you have someone who has been in sales for 30 years and intimately knows all your key accounts?
- What *technology* or *machinery* is your competitive advantage?
- What *material* is your competitive advantage?
- What *process* is your competitive advantage?

We will revisit these questions in the next chapter when we start to develop your knowledge management map. For now, tuck these questions in the back of your mind as you begin to think about what makes your organization stand out from the competition.

Examine Your Organizational Chart

A lot of knowledge is leaving the workplace. It is your job as someone tasked with organizational knowledge management to find it and grab it while you still have it under your roof.

A good succession plan occurs in an organized way, and knowledge management is inextricably linked to a good succession plan. When you marry the contents of your organization's knowledge base with your strategic vision for the enterprise, you can develop a knowledge map that can guide your efforts at preserving what is best and most essential about your business, and use that to guide decisions when choosing people to carry on your mission.

The *Working with SMEs* methodology is a framework for collecting and passing on internal knowledge from individual subject matter experts in an organized way. Those tools, techniques, and templates can help you work with your subject matter experts, but before you do, you need to know with whom you should be speaking and what you need to learn from them.

The *Working with SMEs* methodology includes templates and advice on how to work with subject matter experts, and that is included in the third section of this book. However, before you use those processes, you need to be sure you have found the critical information that you need to be collecting. Analyze your company starting from the top down, and look in the nooks and crannies to find information and people who might not be obvious but are important to your success.

Before you start, study the following diagrams and charts for designing your plan to find your subject matter experts and determine what information you must capture. Get the big picture about where the knowledge capture process is going before you begin. Beginning with the end in mind helps you avoid wasted effort.

This stepwise, planned approach is designed to help you avoid wasted effort collecting information and data that you do not need for business continuity. Go slower to go faster. By thinking ahead of the curve now, you will eliminate taking unnecessary steps later. If your organization is under any kind of threat of imminent loss of knowledge due to retirements, right-sizing, or mergers and acquisitions, you can complete this planning process in about 3–6 months depending on the size of your organization. But if you are operating under such threats, the important task is to begin as soon as you can get your first knowledge discovery meeting scheduled.

Your organization should be concerned about collecting critical knowledge right now. For many companies, a poor economy means the organization is shrinking or being acquired. For others, a more outward-looking global focus and changing technology are shifting the importance of certain types of knowledge – some becoming irrelevant and some more important. Turnover, layoffs, and M&As can also result in loss of important knowledge. Relevant to all organizations, however, is the fact that a lot of the knowledge you need to retain resides in your Baby Boomers who will be retiring soon.

As we saw earlier, workplaces now house five generations. Your knowledge management plan needs to ensure the lines of communication from one to the other are in place. By 2020, it is expected of the five generations in the workplace, the oldest and most experienced will be in the last stages of phasing out. That requires action today. Personally, I have worked with three octogenarians in the past 2 years who are concerned about knowledge preservation.

A strong program for knowledge management and succession planning will inform your training programs and guide purposeful direction to your knowledge management strategy. You need to start by finding out what you need to know, discovering your irreplaceable internal gurus, and then finding out from them what they know and what they do that is critical to your company's survival. List what you could lose when you lose people, and begin to gather their expertise today.

Most companies begin their succession plan by looking for individuals whom they believe can carry on the mission of the organization. When a new leader comes on board, that person is expected to figure out what works, what does not work, and what needs to change. Often, a new employee's first 6 months or more is a treasure hunt no matter whether they are at the helm or calling on customers in your sales department. When you have captured the current wealth of information from those in the know, new employees – including leaders – who come after them can make good decisions based on well-organized information. New line workers find it easier to acclimate to their new tasks when you can provide them with detailed information about how their predecessors succeeded in flawlessly building your product to customer specifications.

This seems obvious, but it would not be stated here unless there are far too many examples of poor execution in this area.

Each organization has a wealth of internal information that needs to be captured and passed on so that the organization can continue its mission. Succession planning linked to knowledge capture is mission critical to your company's survival.

Much is made of change, and change management is a huge area often at the top of mind especially when searching for new leadership.

However, maintaining your core competencies should be at the heart of your training programs. The baby and bathwater metaphor applies when you are making leadership and cultural changes in your organization. One of the mantras of a retiring expert I worked with early in my career applies here, "If it ain't broke, don't fix it."

Your company needs to sustain what it currently does to continue fulfilling its core mission. Those critical pieces, the knowledge, skills, and attitudes that comprise your organization's value and distinction in the marketplace, are the information that you need to capture from your subject matter experts for training and succession planning.

Knowledge management is at the heart of succession planning, and to do it well, you need a plan in place.

Organizational Forgetting

How do you lose important information? There are a lot of deliberate and accidental ways that "Organizational Forgetting" occurs. In an article in Training Industry Magazine, author Tracy Lawrence discusses a framework established by Pablo Martin de Holan and Nelson Philips that identifies the four main ways that we lose institutional knowledge:

1. Memory Decay
2. Failure to Capture
3. Unlearning
4. Avoiding Bad Habits

Furthermore, de Holan and Philips' framework places these four failures along two axes – sources of knowledge and modes of forgetting (Figure 2.1).

A good knowledge management plan and thoughtful succession planning can control for these failures and ultimately avoid these problems. For the purposes of working with experts, I am going to focus on Failure to Capture.

Have a Plan

In the next chapter, you will find exercises to help walk you through a process to identify those things that are in the Critical Information

---

* Based on graphic from *The Implications of Organizational Forgetting*, Tracy Lawrence. Training Industry Magazine. Summer 2014. pp 45–47.

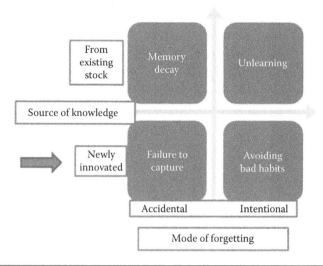

Figure 2.1   Types of organizational forgetting*

domain in your organization – the knowledge that you cannot lose without losing your competitive edge with some or all of your customers. By doing the exercises in the following chapters, you will have a plan for what you need to collect, how to stratify its importance, and with whom you need to be speaking immediately.

This process starts from the top of the organization. Done well, it will lead you to the very bottom rungs of your organization where the employee meets the product, service, and customer every day. From the CEO all the way to the customer, you will uncover valuable information that, if not at the heart of your success, is certainly its veins and arteries.

Nobody can do this exercise for you. If you are a supervisor, manager, or executive in your organization, you cannot outsource this work. Leaders play an important role in knowledge management because without intimate knowledge of your particular industry and your individual corporation, these exercises will not be able to help you peer into every hidden corner. The core of the exercises is to make no assumptions at all, ask everybody good questions, and review with managers, supervisors, and line workers as you create your knowledge management map.

The caveat is that the exercises are only a starting point for your knowledge map. When you get to work and start to implement your plan, be prepared to uncover more people and more information.

When you start asking around and setting up appointments with your internal gurus, expect that the people who know a lot will know where else to look for people and information. And finally, as you continually perform environmental scans of your industry, expect that emerging trends and new technology will change what you perceive to be important. That is why we call the following exercises the *beginning* of your knowledge management plan.

Capture Your Competitive Advantages

Now that you know generally the kind of information and people you will be looking for, let us look at how to dig down and find all those little things that you do every day that give your company its competitive advantage. Once you identify them, the next step is to develop a plan to find the right people so you can capture the internal knowledge, skills, and attitudes that go into the value and distinction that makes you successful in your market.

Your plan's execution depends on having a well-thought-out pathway to discovery. The exercises in this book are intended as the path of your knowledge management plan. When you work through the charts and diagrams provided, you will have identified all the critical pockets of information within your organization so that you can start to excavate that knowledge.

It is possible that you already know, in your head, where those pockets are. Perhaps you have been with the company 30 years and believe that you do not really need to walk through these exercises. Let me suggest that if you are in that position, these exercises are all the more critical to your organization's survival because you are one of the internal subject matter experts on whom your company's survival depends. By doing these exercises, you are leaving plans for those who follow in your footsteps.

Your Value and Distinction

The value and distinction that your company brings to customers is your competitive advantage. Your competitive advantage is the edge over your competition that you cannot afford to lose because therein lies your value. When your competitors reverse engineer your product or service, you have lost your ability to charge a premium for the privilege of offering it uniquely to the public. When you lose your competitive advantage, it drives down the value – and therefore the price – of what your company provides to the marketplace. Therein lies the importance of capturing all those things that make your company distinctive. By capturing and codifying internal expertise, you preserve the value of the asset which is your organization.

> Competitive Advantage: A company's ability to perform in one or more ways that competitors cannot or will not match.*

The textbook definition from Marketing Management by Philip Kotler and Kevin Lane Keller states that your competitive advantage is a company's ability to perform in one or more ways that competitors cannot or will not match.

One caveat is that you cannot assume that you will maintain your competitive edge forever. In fact, assume that you will not. At some point, a competitor will figure out your secret sauce and offer it too, at a lower price, or what you offer will no longer have value in the marketplace. For example, nobody buys cathode ray tubes anymore. Without spending too much time exploring the life cycle of your product or service, suffice it to say that you are looking for your secret sauce – the unique and distinctive value that your company brings to the marketplace – today.

You will find extraordinary value in extrapolating this exercise to include capturing knowledge that may become your competitive advantage sometime in the future. In my research for this book, I came across a study by several university professors that maps the frontiers of the potential for this kind of exercise.

An excellent study published by two University of Pennsylvania professors, Martin Ihrig and Ian Macmillan, discusses how to parse the value of your internal information for its current and future relevance. It is succinctly explained in their article, *Managing Your Mission-Critical Knowledge*, in the January–February 2015 issue of Harvard Business Review. In order to limit and focus *Finding Your SME* exercises here, I will simply reference and recommend it to

---

* Kotler and Keller. Marketing Management 12e, Prentice-Hall of India, 2006.

enrich your knowledge management mapping exercise. In the article, Ihrig and Macmillan discuss how they conducted knowledge capture exercises at companies like Boeing and CERN. Their explanation reveals the depth to which these exercises can be taken within your organization and the kinds of valuable information and relationships among them you may uncover in the process.

As you can see from this simplified reconstruction of Ihrig and Macmillan's diagram on the next page, the most precious knowledge in your organization exists at the intersection of information that is

- Undiffused – it exists only in small, tightly held pockets or by just a handful of people, at most, *and* it is proprietary and essential to the value and distinction that your company brings to the marketplace, and
- Unstructured – it currently is not captured in a stepwise fashion that can be easily transferred to others.

When you move further from undiffused, unstructured information, you find yourself in the land where more people possess the information (diffused) and it is captured in a way that it can be more easily transferred to others (structured). Knowledge that exists further away from that critical intersection of undiffused and unstructured knowledge will include information – the chart example is "worldwide engineering community of practice" – that already can be easily found and accessed by others. You do not need to spend valuable, finite resources capturing this kind of information for your internal training programs to assure your business's continuity.

As you begin to do the exercises in this book to make those determinations, you will ask yourself a series of questions to find the undiffused and unstructured critical information in your organization (Figure 2.2).

For now, we will explore the task of preserving current value and distinction as we define what makes your company special. By knowing the unique value you bring to your customers and what makes your organization distinctive, you will be led directly to the people who know the information that you need to capture to ensure the ongoing survival of your business. On Ihrig and MacMillan's chart, the closer you move toward undiffused and unstructured knowledge, the more closely you need to search for the nuggets of wisdom that you need to capture in this exercise.

A Generic Engineering Company's Knowledge Assets

You can plot your mission-critical knowledge on a map like the one below.

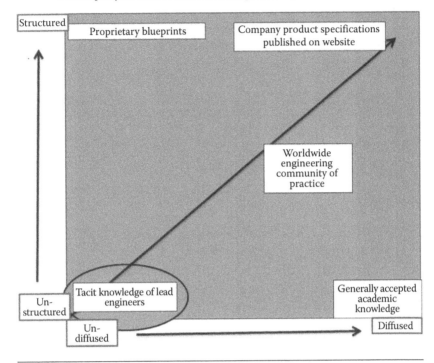

Figure 2.2   What kind of knowledge is this?*

Knowledge Mapping

AUTHOR'S NOTE

While writing this book, I decided to include charts to encourage readers to imagine capturing all your valuable corporate information in a physical format and to see it in a stepwise fashion. No, I don't expect you to fill these out while reading the book! I do not even expect you to recreate these exactly as presented if you decide to run

---

* From the article, *Managing Your Mission-Critical Knowledge,* by Martin Ihrig and Ian MacMillan, January–February 2015 Harvard Business Review, page 7. Diagram adapted and circle added to highlight the kind of knowledge you need to look for when you are *Finding Your SMEs.* This diagram uses a fictitious engineering company as an example.

these exercises. The point of the visual representations throughout this book is to bring order to these ideas that could otherwise be abstract depending on the learning style of the reader. The reader is encouraged to adapt these maps to your own organization for its specific needs and structure.

To begin the knowledge mapping exercise, you can create a map of the big picture describing where your company's knowledge resides. Revisit this list for the kinds of questions you need to ask yourself to begin to complete the first knowledge mapping exercise to identify your competitive advantages.

- What is/are your company's core competency/competencies?
- What are your competitive advantages?
- *Who* is a competitive advantage? Do you have a particularly charismatic or public leader? Do you have someone who is very effective in a customer-facing role?
- What *technology* or *machinery* is your competitive advantage?
- What *material* is your competitive advantage?
- What *process* is your competitive advantage?

The Competitive Advantages map is the basis for all the subsequent exercises so take your time filling it out. Everything that follows will come from this diagram. Think big. Think small. Think creatively. And run this exercise through several layers and filters of the organization using these mapping exercises to involve the perspectives of many other people with both bird's eye and ground level views.

The first person or group who needs to fill out this map has the big picture, someone or some group of people at the top of the organization who has the wide angle view of your company, your industry, and even the larger business environment. An inclusive approach peers into all corners of the organization, and does it in ways that may not always be apparent at ground level.

Conversely, this exercise then needs to run through filters at different layers of the organization, managerial as well as line workers and customer contact employees. Everyone sees the company differently and for this type of exploration, all perspectives have equal value. In

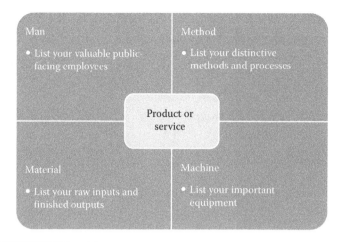

Figure 2.3 Competitive advantages diagram

fact, for some of the essential customer-facing activities, much of the value will be found in the voices on your phone responding to customer inquiries and in the hands clasping briefcases in the lobbies of your potential customers making those ice-breaking customer calls.

Depending on the size and complexity of your organization, you may do this exercise in one session, or you may have a large organization with many layers and divisions, in which case you could run this exercise 10 times or more moving ever closer to the lower functional levels. Only you know your organization, its structure, and how it disperses knowledge.

The point is leave no corner unexplored.

This Competitive Advantages Diagram is based on a common analytic chart called a root cause analysis diagram used to diagnose problems. Its purpose is to make sure all aspects of a situation are considered. There are several versions of this analytic tool, but the one I use here is the most standard version.* Its value in comprehensively diagnosing problems makes it a very good exercise for exploring all aspects of your organization looking for your unique competitive advantages wherever they may be found. Figure 2.3 depicts this

---

* The use of the term "Man" is part of the original root cause analysis diagram; the term "Man" is intended to indicate all humans and no offense is intended to anyone. I use it here to continue the 4M methodology.

common root cause analysis method that you can use to conduct a thorough exploration of where your distinctive corporate assets lie.

How to Complete the Competitive Advantages Diagram

Put the name of your product or service in the middle circle, for example, "health insurance" or "PVC pipe." Your main product or service may have several versions or you may have a few distinct products. Again, use your discretion about whether you can drill down into those areas from one main concept, product, or idea – or if those discrete products and services require separate diagrams. The answer to that question may lie in whether different or related products share manufacturing, leadership, processes, or some other facet of research, development, manufacture, sales, marketing, or supply chain.

The main point is to brainstorm each branch of the core product or service until you have completely run out of ideas. Nothing is too big ("Oh, that's too obvious. Everybody knows that!" Maybe not.) Nothing is insignificant ("She just sweeps the floor. What does she know?" You may be surprised.)

Man Branch: Include the names and roles of people you consider essential to the smooth functioning of your company as you understand it. It may be the CEO or it may be the person who runs the call center with great customer service. It may be the head of marketing who has put together a program that made you highly visible in the community. Think about whom *you* think is essential in the company and their roles. Do not worry about the detail of what they do, why you think they are important, or whether anyone else thinks they are important. We will get to that next. These people may or may not be some of the subject matter experts you will eventually uncover. These are public-facing roles that are competitive advantages to your company in the marketplace in the eyes of your customer. When you dive into identifying subject matter experts for the Man branch, you will uncover the individuals around this valuable corporate asset who actually understand how this person functions.

Material Branch: Consider the physical materials that are essential to your business. If it is health insurance, think about the brochures that are distributed in pharmacies. It might be the design of your retail outlets. If you manufacture a physical consumable, you may think about the inputs and raw materials such as cotton or coal that you need to produce your product. Each of you will see something different because you are looking at the world through your individual lens. That is the value you bring to this exercise. Do not worry about how or why the material is important. At this step, just identify the materials you think make your company distinctive in the marketplace.

Machine Branch: Next, consider the machines that make your company run. It may be the equipment that stamps out parts. It might be the phones. It might be the computers. It might be cars driven by sales people that also serve as mobile billboards. Your perspective is very important here because something you may think is important may not be visible to someone else in another part of the organization.

Method Branch: Finally, consider the methods and processes that are essential to making your company run. If you are in accounting, it may be the accounting system. If you are in customer service, it could be the software that you use to register and track customers. If you are in the training department, it could be the learning management system. Describe the processes with which you are familiar in your part of the company that are essential for its day-to-day functioning. Again, bear in mind that no one else has your unique view of your business so assume you are seeing things of value that are not in the line of sight of people in other parts of the business.

The Value of the Exercise

Run this exercise at every level of your organization and through anyone who has any knowledge of your customers and what you do to bring value to the marketplace. The essence of this exercise is that everyone's point of view is important. People are each looking at your organization in a different way, and any person's perspective is as important as any other's. Keep an open mind about involving people, and keep that same open mind about what they say. Often the most unlikely people possess the most critical knowledge.

This exercise is your first filter to finding that information. Everything is important at this stage. Later exercises will help you determine what stays, what goes, and where else you may need to look.

Your motto for the Competitive Advantages Diagram exercise can be "It is all good!"

3

SUCCESSION PLANNING
WITH YOUR SMEs

The more comprehensively you completed the Competitive Advantages Four M Exercise will determine the success of your efforts to find your subject matter experts at all subsequent phases. After you have uncovered the essential and critical assets related to your products and services, you can begin to uncover your experts.

Name Your Gurus

If you think you are done slicing and dicing your organization, think again! You have only just begun. Now you can take what you have learned by identifying your assets and running them through a different type of sieve, which is the sieve of your functional areas. That is where you will find the people who are your experts related to the critical components you identified as one of your competitive advantages. The point of *Finding Your SMEs* is to leave no stone unturned, so now we will essentially cross-hatch the analysis of your organizational assets using a different focus.

When you are trying to find your subject matter experts, you need to look at your organizational chart. If you have a small and simple organization, much of this is intuitive and you are not likely to need another layer of discovery. However, if your organization has any level of complexity, it may serve you to consider running this as an actual deep dive exercise with members of your initial discovery group involved in the Competitive Advantages Diagram Exercise.

So far, you have drilled down into four areas, man, machine, method, and material. Logically, you could conclude that the Man portion of the knowledge mapping exercise located your subject matter experts. That is only partially true.

In the Man portion of the exercise, you are looking for people who are the face of the organization to the public, either the general public for public relations and marketing purposes, or they are the face of your organization to your customers. They are your essential and critical assets and part of your competitive advantage. They are recognized faces attached to your organization's capability either internally or externally, but their expertise is only part of the picture. The people around them, who are the experts about them, are just as important for the next exercise.

For this next part of your mission to search for expertise in your organization, you are going to look at the critical Man, Method, Machine, and Materials assets that you have identified and find the people who are experts in those areas. Those people are your internal subject matter experts.

If you have a small organization, most of this may be intuitive and you may think it is superfluous to run an exercise to map a chart to find them. However, you need to run these exercises and commit these names to a map no matter how small your organization. Your treasure might be more easily found in a small company, but you still need to leave a treasure map for those who come after you.

When you have a complex organization of perhaps a 1,000 people or more – you will know best whether you need to do this – it is a good idea to create your map by running this exercise through several layers of the organization. If you have an organization of 1,000 people and many of them are warehouse workers doing similar work, you may not need to drill down too deeply in that unit. However, if you are a high-tech firm employing 1,000 engineers and other knowledge workers, you will probably need to execute the next step very carefully because each worker may have highly disparate knowledge.

When you are ready to name your gurus, you will be finding individuals, not roles or titles. You may find some of your Machine, Method, Man, and Material experts in your organization may not even have a title. They are sometimes the researchers in labs or the engineers poring over software design, and this next exercise will help you locate them.

About the Functional Area Exercise

In order to locate individual experts, think about the structure of your company and your organizational chart. I recommend creating a chart similar to the one in this section, *Identify SMEs by Functional Area and Role.*

You are looking for people who know and work with the critical items identified in your Competitive Advantages Diagram Four M Exercise. You now need to systematically go through the list of critical assets you have identified and tie them to specific people in functional areas of your enterprise. For example, if you have named a certain machine as a critical asset, consider who might know about its cost (accounting and finance) and its maintenance schedule (the floor supervisor) as well as the actual operator. For material inputs, consider accounting and finance, logistics, and R&D as possible sources of information about a critical material asset – what does it cost, how and where do you source it, can it be substituted with something else, and so on.

To create such a chart for your own organization, think about these questions:

For the X axis across the top: What are your major functional areas?

For the Y axis along the left side: What are the roles in each functional area?

It will look like this sample in Figure 3.1.

Role	Management & Leadership	Manufacturing	R&D	Sales & Marketing	Logistics (Warehouse, transportation)
CEO/SVP/VP					
Manager					
Manager					
Supervisor					
Supervisor					
Veteran Employee					
Veteran Employee					

Figure 3.1 Identify SMEs by functional area and role

Please note that this is just an example about how to construct this exercise because your chart will probably have different functional areas, roles, and titles.

Your task in filling out the Functional Area and Role Chart is to name individuals. When you are through, you should have the names of people in the boxes.

When filling in this chart for specific leadership and managerial roles, consider:

- Who currently fills the role?
- Who has filled the role recently?
- Who is being groomed to fill the role?

When you are filling in this chart and looking for knowledgeable employees, consider:

- Who has been around the longest?
- Who is most likely to leave within the next 6–12 months?
- Who is the recognized expert in that department?
- Who holds proprietary process information and knowledge such as accounting processes, marketing approach, vendor management, legal expertise, and so on?

Consider creating subsections of this chart to include people who have roles in the present, the immediate past, and those who are in line for positions.

When you have filled out the Functional Area and Role Chart, you are well on your way to identifying all the people holding the critical information in your organization. In most medium-sized or larger organizations, you may still uncover a few experts when you are interviewing the people on this chart. But for the most part, consider that the names on this chart are your main target subject matter experts.

Good work. You are getting there.

The Reluctant SME

Do not be surprised if you find that some of your internal subject matter experts are not enthusiastic about sharing their knowledge with you. In fact, be surprised if all of them are willing to do so. People do not like to consider themselves replaceable and may feel threatened.

First, some union workers consider their skills their own proprietary knowledge and not the property of your organization. Some workers believe that you are hiring their expertise and by telling you what they know, they are devaluing the skills they bring to the table. It may even be against some union or guild rules to share certain information with you. This is not an easy situation to resolve. Your goal is to gather only information specific to your company's critical assets as part of your corporate body of knowledge, so this applies solely to expertise your employees have about your proprietary and critical assets and infrastructure. It is a good idea to have managers at all levels who are experts in all your critical assets if this is your situation. Single managers cannot reasonably be expected to run a plant in lieu of union workers, and let me emphasize that is not the point of the exercise. Again, this is a sensitive subject, and it is not the goal of this exercise to put union workers – or any workers – out of a job. But this could be one issue that arises as you look for veteran line workers who have access to competitive information and knowledge about critical assets that are essential to business continuity. If this is the case, you might have to negotiate with the union, guild, or some other employee representative to speak with those workers. Be aware of this issue.

Even those workers who are not covered by a guild or union may feel somewhat threatened by telling you what they know. They may be suspicious about why you are asking them detailed questions about their functions and knowledge, and they may wonder if you are trying to put them out of a job or replace them. Because workers can be competitive and suspicious, this can thwart your information gathering efforts.

When you undertake an exercise like this with employees, you need to be clear with them that you are gathering information to complete your training programs and that nobody's job is being eliminated as a result of this exercise. Reassure them about how important they are to your organization, and it is the very fact that they cannot be easily replaced or that what they know takes years to acquire that you are involving them in this critical information gathering exercise. You may want to incentivize them to be involved in training and mentoring to reinforce their stature in the organization. In fact, it is wise to cross-train employees, and this step is important when you are instituting a cross-training initiative. If you have a larger corporation where you anticipate you may end up talking to a few hundred people over the course of several months or more, you might consider doing an internal communications program explaining what you are doing and why you are doing it to eliminate gossip and fear mongering among employees.

When you find people within your organization who have proprietary knowledge about your products and services and are reluctant to share it, you have learned that you have a vulnerability in that area. The company needs to have full access to information about all processes, products, and services you provide. If you find that some workers' reluctance to share their knowledge leaves a gap in your knowledge map, you then need to assess how to handle that situation to reduce your exposure to losing that critical asset.

You may consider:

1. Managers job-shadow critical functions
2. Training departments ask Reluctant SMEs to act as mentors, teachers, and classroom facilitators for additional compensation or recognition
3. Implement safety or other regulatory reviews of positions to assess them for compliance. (If you are not sure how something is done, you want to compel your employees to cooperate to ensure that role is meeting whatever codes and requirements your company is obliged to adhere to.)

It is beyond the scope of this book to explore these options because this can be a complex human resources situation, but it is worth mentioning that you may uncover The Reluctant SME, and it is a situation you will need to address to protect your business continuity plan.

In the third section of this book, we explore how to handle challenging situations when working with subject matter experts including more advice on working with The Reluctant SME.

The most important takeaway at this point is that your experts are the key to your organizational survival. Learning who they are and how to work with them is part of your business continuity plan.

Your SME Catch and Release Program: The Process of Retirement and Rehirement

Timing is one of the most important aspects of finding and capturing knowledge from your retiring subject matter experts. When you are prioritizing where to concentrate your finite time and resources, consider your experts' seniority and expected tenure. If you think a long-term employee is going to leave in the next 6–12 months or has already announced their retirement, obviously those people need to go to the head of the line when you start your knowledge collection process.

It is possible you may realize that you are losing valuable knowledge that you cannot reasonably capture and retain in a short period of time, if at all. I have seen that case with a very highly regarded and experienced biochemical engineer. He was just irreplaceable. Period. In order to capture as much of his knowledge, skills, and attitudes as possible from him, and because he was a truly dedicated employee who loved the company, the company was able to hire him back as a consultant – and make it worth his while. Be prepared to do that and to pay handsomely to do it with extremely valuable individuals.

STORYTIME

The case of the irreplaceable biochemical engineer is worth recounting because it shows not only how to handle this situation very well, but it is also helpful to describe the kinds of qualities that have value beyond an employee's tenure and are worth capturing. This particular engineer embodied the qualities of an employee who made himself irreplaceable – and those qualities were worth replicating.

It was not just what John (not his real name) knew, although he knew virtually everything there was to know about the company's sophisticated product line, product development, and manufacturing. He understood the company values and culture. He literally walked within the safety walkways.

John was extremely intelligent and kind, and to use a well-worn phrase, he forgot more than most people will ever know about his company's products, processes, and history. After he officially retired, the company hired him back as a highly valued consultant. He worked to build an intricate training program – in fact they called it a university – to capture and transfer not only product and process knowledge, but to try to capture the thinking skills that went into decision-making at all levels of the organization.

He brought one more asset to the table. He put himself on the floor with line workers and got into the details of their learning. He epitomized the humble servant. It was not just what he knew that made him valuable. It was his demeanor and the way he carried himself. He embodied the dignity, humor, gentleness, and honesty of the best the organization had to offer. He was the walking definition of integrity. His service beyond his employment helped carry forward corporate values and culture in a way that only someone with his tenure, seniority, and depth could possibly have done.

If you have a John who is ready to retire, he is worth keeping around – if you can.

Special Section: Succession Planning for Family-Owned Businesses

Small, family-owned and other privately, closely held companies are some of the most vulnerable to extinction when they lose their expertise. Largely, this is because the founder is often the main subject matter expert, as well as the company president and CEO. When the founder chooses to retire, pass the business to heirs, or unexpectedly becomes ill or passes away, a business that relies on that single person's knowledge and business connections can quickly deteriorate.

Many books have been written on this topic, and there are dedicated experts in the field of succession planning for family-owned businesses. This section is not intended to replace any of that wisdom, but rather just to remind the reader that this type of business has a specific type of vulnerability to the loss of expertise that needs to be dealt with differently than capturing knowledge from subject matter experts in large, publicly-held companies.

Here are tales of two similar small, family-held companies that were losing their founder and CEO, but each company has a very different outcome. In both cases, I was brought in to ghostwrite books for the CEOs, so I am familiar with the details but am masking them to preserve their privacy.

The Engineering Whiz: A Founder's Succession Planning

Measurement Engineering was founded by an engineer who perfected a process for measuring bulk liquids and dry material. He built a company of 200 dedicated employees, most of whom were technologists and other engineers. He was a strong, intelligent, and humane leader who built a vibrant corporate culture that respected workers and delivered exemplary service in the field.

As the founder approached retirement, his son, who was also an engineer with the company, said he had no desire to run it. The founder hired an executive search firm who engaged a recently retired military officer with the human resource and administrative background to safely steer the company into the future, while the son happily remained head of engineering and took his place on the board of directors. The company still thrives 30 years after the founder retired.

The Cement King: Wresting Control from the Heirs

As the industrial revolution got underway in the beginning of the 20th century, the Colonel took his early investment in a manufacturing company that made car wheels and axles and converted his earnings into a company that built cement factories. Under his guidance and passion, the Colonel created a respected, global business that rode the wave of industrial development into the 1940s and 1950s. Upon his retirement, his three sons showed no interest in running the family business but also had no desire to give up the family golden goose. Or rather the goose it had become under their father.

The sons' interest in polo and sailing far outweighed their interest in manufacturing cement plants, and the company eventually was operating at a loss and in danger of bankruptcy. Finally, some members of the board of directors insisted on hiring new management over the objections of the sons. A global search company secured the service of a seasoned executive with exceptional experience in turning around failing business units.

The new CEO upended the lax corporate culture, renewed relationships with unsatisfied customers, and with the company's improved reputation, was able to attract new business around the globe. He took the company from 3% to 34% of global market share in only 4 years. The revived company soared in value and eventually was acquired by its main competitor.

Less Happy Endings

Some small, privately-held companies have less happy endings with one, two, or more generations of the founder's hard work eventually destroyed by uninvolved, incompetent, or greedy heirs. The history of business is littered with poorly managed family succession plans. Often, it is the children or wife of the founder who are/is unwilling or unable to make good decisions about continuity planning.

This does not have to happen.

If you are the founder or current owner of a small business upon whom its customers and employees depend, it is best to plan early and often to capture what is essential for business continuity. As the founder/president/CEO of a small business, you are the main subject matter expert in your company. Your depth and breadth of knowledge about all parts of the business far outpace simple knowledge capture. So start early, participate in cataloging everything, and make sure you have a few confidantes who can backstop you in the event you decide to indefinitely extend your vacation in Bali.

As a small business owner, the best time to start planning for your exit is at the very beginning of your venture. To avoid having your business tossed on the rubbish pile of history, you can take a few steps.

1. Plan from the beginning to capture important knowledge in a way that is easily found, retrieved, and applied
2. Put supports in place for your corporate culture that extend beyond yourself. This is important for employees as well as for customers who have come to expect to be treated a certain way – the way that keeps them coming back.
3. Double or triple yourself and the other essential people in your organization.
4. Cross-train everybody.
5. Have a clear exit strategy or have legal documents in place that clearly spell out who does what, who gets what, and how

things are split. (My uncle and his business partner had an agreement drawn up that whoever died first, the other would buy out the partner's half of their manufacturing firm and remit the proceeds to the decedent's wife.)

As auto accidents and heart attacks prove every day, we cannot always plan a graceful exit. Caring for what happens without you is part of the stewardship of your business asset and an act of responsibility toward your employees, your family, and your customers.

4

THE EXPERTS' DISCERNMENT

So far, you have figured out your competitive advantages and drilled down to determine the identities of your most critical human assets – your subject matter experts. After you have identified them and before you begin to work with them to download their valuable corporate knowledge, you need to engage them to determine the information that is most critical to your corporate future. As experts, they have the catbird seat when it comes to knowing what information is most critical and irreplaceable, and what valuable internal knowledge assets can be reproduced or found elsewhere without them.

The first task of your experts is to help you parse the difference among your critical, essential, and non-essential information so your content gathering efforts are spent where they are most needed.

Prioritize and Organize Your Assets

The greatest danger in knowledge management is that you think nothing is important enough to take this amount of effort to preserve. The second greatest danger is that you think everything is important and you become overwhelmed. Now it is time to prioritize what you have found and make those judgment calls.

At this point, you need to sort out the knowledge, skills, and atti-tudes that make your organization valuable to its customers. You will need to return to the people who were part of your Competitive Advantages Diagram group for this one last portion of their task. With this group in place, you can begin to prioritize and organize information for your subject matter experts to identify what is impor-tant that cannot be lost to time or attrition.

You have assembled a comprehensive view of the knowledge within your organization, and you can begin to stratify it to determine what you must capture for business continuity. Identify each item your group has uncovered under each of the four categories – man, machine, materials, and methods – and assign each bit of knowledge into one of the three following categories: non-essential, essential, and critical. To think it through, you can use a chart similar to the ones that follow to discriminate among the three types of information using the definitions* found below.

Identifying Critical Assets: Your Value and Distinction

Let us visit the concepts of non-essential, essential, and critical knowledge, skills and attitudes. The concepts of non-essential, essential, and critical only apply to that particular knowledge that makes your company unique in the marketplace. These categories exist to help you find your critical subject matter experts within your organization whom you cannot lose without also losing information that gives your company its competitive advantage.

You need training for all types of information – non-essential, essential, and critical. It is all important for business continuity. However, for the purposes of capturing organizational knowledge from your internal subject matter experts, you are looking only for the knowledge, skills, and attitudes that define your brand and cannot be replicated elsewhere. In the language of business, your critical knowledge is your competitive advantage. Ask yourself, "What makes our company special to our customers and different from our competitors?" What can they not get anywhere else? That is the critical knowledge you need to capture.

Non-essential information is the information that makes your business function optimally, but it is not particular to your organization. Without this information, your business can survive but it may not thrive. This is the kind of information and knowledge that, done well, makes your business more successful or profitable. But without it, you still have a sufficient and viable differentiated product. For example, leadership optimization programs are often in this realm of knowledge. You may clunk along for years with suboptimal leadership performance. It would be nice to improve the organization, but it will not be essential to getting a sufficient Funburger out the door.

---

* These definitions are my own developed for the process of discovering your company's unique value that your company brings to the marketplace that cannot or should not be able to be replicated by competitors.

In the next round of analysis, you will be able to remove this type of information from consideration. Right now, identify and categorize it to acknowledge it for your records.

Example: Your lists of professional associations and annual meetings.

Rationale: Not every business in your industry attends professional meetings or joins associations, and no business must do it. However, those who belong to such organizations are usually superior performers and leaders in their industries. *You do not need internal subject matter expertise to acquire or maintain this type of knowledge. It is non-essential to your organization's survival and not particular to your organization.*

Essential information is the kind of knowledge that is required for you to do business. It includes things like software such as your productivity suite. It includes your accounting procedures. It also includes things like OSHA compliance training or other regulatory and industry standards that are necessary to do business in your sector. This kind of information is essential for you to do business, but it is not particular to your organization. Other businesses in your industry have the same or similar requirements and usually anyone can come in from another company in your industry and provide it, learn it, or adapt to it easily.

While essential information is the kind of knowledge required for you to do business, it is not particular to your organization. Essential information is retained on your chart in the next round. While you will not need your internal subject matter experts for business continuity for this category of information, you will want to make sure it is recorded and available for transfer.

Example: Federal regulations regarding human resource management and EEOC requirements.

Rationale: Every business in your industry must retain this information in order to do business, but it is not company-specific. *You do not need internal subject matter experts to acquire or maintain this type of knowledge.*

Focus on Critical Information

Critical information makes your company unique. This is the place where you want to capture most of the knowledge from your internal experts. Critical information includes the software that is developed specifically for your company, or if you are a software company, the software developed specifically by your company. It includes how to manufacture your proprietary products, such as your pills, if you are a pharmaceutical company or what goes into the futuristic building material that you make for green industrial projects if you are in the construction industry. Whatever it is that you do that is unique to your company – we call it the value and distinction that you bring to your customers – that is the critical information that you must capture. It is not just the diagrams for your patented product that you need to capture; you need to capture all the people, systems, materials, and processes that support the entire enterprise from end to end that are unique to your company. Those are all the bits of knowledge that you need to preserve when you are looking to collect information from your subject matter experts.

The danger is that you assume you already know this information. Do not make that assumption. Instead, do a thorough analysis that walks down the path of each business unit and searches for golden nuggets. You will find a few, maybe more. You are looking not only for the known critical information that defines your company's niche; you also want to uncover those hidden nuggets that are not commonly known. This critical information is the place where you want to capture most of the knowledge from your internal experts. In the language of Ihrig and MacMillan, this knowledge is undiffused.

Examples:

- Your patented products and processes
- Trademarks and copyrighted materials
- Proprietary lists of customers and suppliers

Keep thinking about what is uniquely yours that would be difficult or impossible to replicate when retaining or building on your competitive advantages.

Rationale: No other company in your industry has – or should have – this information or asset. That is why *you need to speak with your internal subject matter experts about your critical assets.*

STORYTIME

One financial department of a huge global corporation is based in the quiet hills in the northeast U.S. For 40 years, it has been run by a local ethnic man, let's call him Joe. Joe has ties to the community and a practical, no-nonsense but kind manner. His department is mostly populated with people like him, people who have a strong and honest work ethic and an understanding of human nature. His department ran collections for a health-care firm. Competitor firms ran their collection departments according to common practice with phone banks and scripted banter. Not this guy. His handpicked group of callers over time have come to know each customer, each mom and pop physician's office that purchases products. They know each customer's income, outgo, revenue cycles, the issues with particular patients, you name it. The goal of Joe's finance department is not just to collect overdue accounts; the goal of each person in the division under Joe's guidance is to get lifesaving products into the hands of physicians in an uninterrupted flow so they can treat patients. The collectors know whom to talk to, what to ask, how much to ask for, and when things might pick up so they can zero out the bill. Is this exceptional? Yes. While virtually every other similar company in the industry has dismal collection records, his company is flush with cash from his efforts. Before Joe leaves, he has a lot of secrets of interpersonal relationships, management techniques, bookkeeping adjustments, and industry knowledge to share. He makes good judgment calls almost every time. You might say it is Joe's instinct, but instinct is often just experience over time until your gut knows.

MORAL OF THE STORY

You cannot teach in one day the kind of experience over time that becomes instinct. But you can capture some of the guidelines and parameters Joe has developed either unofficially or in documentation, preserve it, and pass it on. The secret to capturing instinctive knowledge is to watch Joe do his job and look for the things he might not think to mention. Joe is an unconscious competent; he knows more than he knows he knows. Those unspoken nuggets are the things that are instinct to Joe...and priceless knowledge to the company.

Knowledge Stratification

After you have identified all your assets, it is time to take the massive amounts of internal information you have collected and list the information that you need to preserve using the non-essential, essential, and critical filters.

Assuming you have focused on a big picture overview of your product or service, it is time to drill down deeper into the details of that product. If you have a large company, this task can be overwhelming so it may have to be broken out by business units, locations, or departments. But for the purpose of this book, I am keeping it relatively simple and assuming this can be done with a few rounds of analysis with a few knowledgeable individuals. Only you know if your company is large and complex enough to break this out further by geography, business units, product lines, and so on.

Knowledge Stratification: Look at your Competitive Advantages Diagram. If you have a small organization, you can probably do this exercise in one quick pass. If this is the case, do not worry about whether your assets fit into the man, machine, method, or material category because you can probably include them on one chart and perform one general analysis of your company assets. Look at the assets you have identified and decide whether the most important bits of information fit into the non-essential, essential, or critical category.

However, if you have a large or complex organization and have identified hundreds or thousands of bits of discrete knowledge on a first indiscriminate pass, you can conduct Knowledge Stratification and complete the subsequent Knowledge and Training Gap Analysis by breaking it down into the man, method, machine, and material categories. For the purposes of this book, I am going to break out the knowledge stratification exercise by man, machine, method, or material to explain the logic behind identifying critical assets.

Note: If you have a small company with only one or two products, you may not need to go any further than this core exercise because it will be apparent which subject matter experts are attached to your critical assets on the first pass. Include all the assets from the man, method, machine, and material arms if you fill out one general chart.

Find Knowledge and Training Gaps

After you have completed the knowledge stratification chart, figure out if your company already has essential and critical knowledge captured and catalogued somewhere so it can be passed on. Look for this information in your training department if you have one. If you do, you may find much of this information housed within the training function. If you do not have a training department, knowledge is probably captured and transferred by managers and supervisors, so you can start searching for it there.

Checklist: Find Your Knowledge and Training Gaps

Identify existing assets

- Job aids
- Diagrams and schematics
- Checklists
- Formal training programs
- OJT by word-of-mouth or personal demonstration

You may also find no formal guidance or organization of your assets but rather an informal system of knowledge transfer. In some cases, you will find no systematic knowledge transfer at all. If you find chaos, now is the time to bring order to the work. Consider this exercise an opportunity to capture important knowledge where no formal or informal system exists for performing a task or passing it on in an organized way.

The Knowledge and Training Gap Exercise is the place where you remove the items that you have identified as "non-essential" from the work stream. Those non-essential items can be easily acquired outside your organization at any time so you do not need to spend valuable internal resources to capture and retain them. Non-essential information can be acquired externally on an as-needed basis. You included it on the first pass to establish a historical record that it exists, and you have put it through a sieve of discrimination exercises to determine that it is not worth spending resources to preserve. While it is important to acknowledge and document your non-essential assets, they will not be relevant from this point forward as it relates to working with your subject matter experts.

This Knowledge and Training Gap Exercise is about finding the important assets that make your company distinctive. At this point, you are finding where and how important internal knowledge is currently stored. For the purpose of finding and working with your indispensable internal subject matter experts, there are two types of knowledge that are part of your organizational survival, essential and critical. When you make decisions about spending resources to capture, retain. and transfer that knowledge, you will ultimately only be concerned with speaking with subject matter experts that hold your corporate critical information.

To conduct this exercise, transfer the essential and critical information you identified in the Knowledge Stratification Exercise to this Knowledge and Training Gap Chart.

As stated earlier, if you have a small organization, you will probably be able to capture all the assets from the man, machine, method, and materials arms of the Competitive Advantages Diagram on one pass in this exercise. If not, you may want to conduct this exercise for each arm of the diagram.

How to Prioritize the 4 Ms

Drill Down into Target Area Man

One of the reasons for the up to 80% failure rate of succession plans is that companies are trying to replace an individual. The organization is worried about the loss of a particularly charismatic or public leader. The mistake is trying to replace someone who is irreplaceable. When that person leaves the role, the qualities and characteristics that the new leader must embody will be different. You cannot replace Steve Jobs. He will forever be the face of Apple. You cannot replace Bill Gates. He will forever be the face of Microsoft. Smaller, lesser known companies also have had equally high-profile leaders within their industry or community that left similar legacies.

As the continued profitability of the companies testifies, the loss of those leaders did not mean the loss of market share. In fact, new and different leadership is often appropriate at certain points in the growth of a company. But the loss of charismatic leaders could possibly leave employees adrift in a cultural no man's land.

Leadership and Influence Is throughout Your Company

When you lose a Steve Jobs, it is obvious. The world notices. If you are in a smaller, less public-facing company, internal leadership and your industry notices when you lose an influential leader.

The main point of this section – and this book – is that that some kind of critical loss of important individuals is happening throughout your organization, not just at the very top. And for the purposes of this part of the analysis, we are going to be most concerned about the impact of the loss of those employees on business continuity.

Critical personnel loss is happening throughout your organization all the time because the place the actual work is done is where most of your customers are experiencing your business. It is not all that uncommon that you have someone in the accounting department for the last 40 years who has been quietly doing his or her job, interfacing with your critical accounts, who knows the details of your customers' financial cycles (see Storytime). That employee has been working with your customers over the phone, sending out reminders that they need in a way they need them, and making adjustments in their collections approach that has kept cash flowing into your organization.

When that person retires and the replacement tries to impose the rules he or she has learned in business school for interfacing with accounts, those long nurtured relationships will be forever altered. Unless, of course, you know who those people in your accounting department are, you know what they have learned, and you are working with their replacements to ease the transition.

Fill out the man arm of your chart with people or roles in your organization who are in pivotal spots. You do not need to include everyone or every role, but you do need to include visible people performing core functions. You might list a good machine operator who has been with you 5 or more years, but you might not include his assistant. At this point, you will include anyone who visibly performs a core function. You will decide later if that person needs to be included as an expert, so do not worry about making that decision yet.

Prioritize and Organize Your Man Assets

Based on the above discussion, decide which man or woman is non-essential, essential or, critical.

With input from your group, list your identified people into three categories on your table chart (Figure 4.1).

The Knowledge and Training Gap Exercise

After you have completed the Knowledge Stratification drill down, figure out if you already have that person's knowledge captured and catalogued somewhere so it can be passed on. In this case, your

Knowledge collection	Non-essential	Essential	Critical

Figure 4.1   Prioritize and organize your knowledge collection – man assets

assets are individuals and the knowledge gaps are the types of information they already may have developed that leave clues about what they do.

Find Your Gaps

Identify existing assets

- Speeches, slides, and video lectures
- Professional and peer-reviewed journal articles and books
- Job aids
- Diagrams and schematics
- Checklists
- Formal training program
- No formal guidance
- OJT by word-of-mouth or personal demo

Next, you will transfer the names of people or the roles you have identified as essential or critical in the prior exercise onto this worksheet. Then identify what, if anything, is currently codified or how their knowledge is passed on (Figure 4.2).

Essential	Critical	No information; OJT	Job aids, diagrams, checklists	Formal training program

Figure 4.2   Identify training gaps – man assets

Drill Down into Target Area Machine

Depending on the type of business or industry you are in, this could be the most crucial part of the exercise. For example, in manufacturing enterprises, this is where a lot of the work – and the problems – arise in cataloguing your mission critical assets. It is not uncommon for highly specialized manufacturing companies to have equipment that has been modified to meet certain customer specifications. In some cases, legacy and proprietary equipment is almost, literally, irreplaceable. The kinds of hands-on mechanical knowledge that built, and even more importantly maintains, the equipment is rare and getting rarer. When I talk to companies who are concerned about preserving their knowledge base, people often talk about the difficulty of replacing legacy equipment and the people who run it.

When you are thinking about machines, consider the forklifts, trucks, vehicle fleet, and pneumatic devices that are part of operations too.

Computers and More

Proprietary corporate computers that housed internal private data are slowly dying out. In their place, companies are starting to be comfortable with secure, cloud-based information systems. The transition has been slow and is hardly complete. For many businesses, this is a common example of having to either maintain or replace outdated equipment and outmoded ways of doing business. Those who have been around long enough – like me – remember running companies on the old DEC (Digital Equipment Corporation) mainframes, and we know that the transitions to PCs or the cloud are often slow and painful. Some are still making those changes, but more commonly, businesses have completed the transition to a more flexible computing environment.

Similar dilemmas are facing manufacturing companies who are producing goods on equipment that may have been built in the 1960s or even earlier. Some companies are keeping those machines running with rubber bands and duct tape, metaphorically speaking (usually!). One of the crises I often hear is that it is hard to find technical workers to learn the intricacies and peculiarities of legacy equipment. For some particular requirements, the existing machinery meets a need very difficult to replicate with other technology. Manufacturers report a dearth of young workers willing, capable, or both to learn how to operate their legacy equipment.

A problem that runs in tandem with finding ready and willing machine operators is the difficulty finding the skill, talent, and knowledge accumulated to maintain them. I have a friend who makes a very good living driving around the Mid-Atlantic and New England states repairing one very specific, outdated machine that needs a lot of coaxing to continue to run. He knows where to tap, what the sounds mean, what the smells mean, and can interpret that into a successful repair. Over a career spanning nearly 50 years, he has found one other person he can send out in place of himself. He ponders writing manuals so the machine operators can troubleshoot issues without him, but he says that solution has limited utility if the operator is young and inexperienced.

Ultimately, much of the equipment that was the bedrock of the post-World War II manufacturing industry will go the way of the DEC mainframe to be replaced by robotics, 3D printers, or some other yet to be developed technology. For now, and for the purpose of keeping your business running, it is important to identify the machinery that is currently critical to fill your customers' orders.

Of course, for businesses that have fully transitioned to future state technology, it is just as important to list that equipment, if not more so. You want that high tech equipment to function optimally and be around awhile so you can recoup your significant investment in it.

Prioritize and Organize Your Information

Based on the above discussion, decide which Machines are non-essential, essential, or critical.

With your group, list those machines or equipment into three categories on this chart (Figure 4.3).

The Knowledge and Training Gap Exercise

After you have completed the Knowledge Stratification Exercise, figure out if you already have the assets to operate, maintain, and replace your equipment captured and catalogued somewhere so it can be passed on.

Knowledge collection	Non-essential	Essential	Critical

Figure 4.3   Prioritize and organize knowledge collection – machine assets

Whether or not you have a training department, you will find much of this information outside the formal training function. Look for a lot of this information at work stations, taped to the equipment itself, or in the drawers and on the walls of supervisors and managers, and sometimes people higher in the organization.

Find Your Gaps

Identify existing assets

- Job aids
- Diagrams and schematics
- Checklists
- Formal training program
- No formal guidance
- OJT by word-of-mouth or personal demonstration

Essential	Critical	No information; OJT	Job aids, diagrams, checklists	Formal training program

Figure 4.4   Identify training gaps – machine assets

Next, you will transfer the equipment that you have identified as essential or critical onto this list and itemize the types of information you currently have at your disposal about that equipment. For many companies, this list may be very long. You might consider doing this exercise in a spreadsheet if you have a lot of equipment and variables regarding its operation and maintenance (Figure 4.4).

Drill Down into Target Area Materials

This exercise may be linked in your mind to the machines that you use to operate your business and build your products because you think of material as either inputs or outputs. It is important to identify the materials that are unique to your enterprise. You can think about material from two perspectives: (1) the material outputs you produce to sell (for example, fabric, gasses, and metals) and (2) the essential material inputs to build your products or offer your services (for example, minerals and raw foods).

When a Common Material May Not Be So Common

One of the stratification exercises asks you to name non-essential versus essential and critical assets. It is here that you will need to make a judgment about whether your common material, which you may be tempted to list as non-essential, is actually critical. Some non-essential materials may be water and power (gas and so on). They are commonly expected to be baseline materials that are relatively reliable where you have chosen to locate your business.

However, you may have a particular business need where your utilization is unusual. You may use extraordinary amounts of water for one of your processes, perhaps fabric dying, for example. In that case, your water usage and water rights are critical to the operation of your business. That means this otherwise common resource will be an extraordinary and critical material for your business. If you have a material like that, think about how easy it would be to replace and whether interruption of the availability of that material could disrupt production or functioning.

The Materials You Produce

The unique metals, fabrics, solvents, solutions, or brochures and CDs are the materials you make to sell. They belong on this list, too, and usually are in the critical column. Theoretically, for the purposes of this exercise, only you can produce them. They often have some kind of intellectual property condition attached to them such as a registered trademark, patent, or copyright. When another company reverse engineers or duplicates your distinct material for sale, you lose your competitive advantage.

The inputs, people's knowledge, skills, and abilities and the machines to produce them are all part of the exercises here. However, it is important to name the product you make, if you make a product, here.

Prioritize and Organize Your Information

Based on the above discussion, which material is non-essential, essential or critical?

Knowledge collection	Non-essential	Essential	Critical

Figure 4.5   Organize and prioritize knowledge – material assets

With your group, list the materials you have identified into three categories on this chart (Figure 4.5).

The Knowledge and Training Gap Exercise

After you have completed the Knowledge Stratification Exercise, figure out if you already have the knowledge related to that material captured and catalogued somewhere so it can be passed on.

For material inputs, think about your suppliers, their contact information, and any special arrangements that you have with them regarding price, delivery, warehousing, quality controls, and so on. For your own products, consider any instruction manuals, warnings, or required labeling that must accompany the product. Where is that information kept? How is it indexed or filed? Who keeps it up-to-date? Is it provided in many languages, and if so, who is responsible for that? If you will recall the graphic that depicts the importance of undiffused and unstructured knowledge in Chapter 2, public manuals that describe the product are structured and diffused, meaning that the documents themselves are easily available and easy to follow. That might suggest that they can be relegated to non-essential information. However, consider whether there is something about them – the vendor who produces them or some particular feature about their distribution for example – that might be difficult to replicate. If that is the case, you may still need to find your expert attached to that otherwise seemingly easily replicable document.

As with the machine exercise above, you may be in a business that uses an extraordinary amount of material inputs, in which case you might consider doing this exercise in spreadsheet software (Figure 4.6).

Essential	Critical	No information; OJT	Job aids, diagrams, checklists	Formal training program

Figure 4.6   Identify training gaps

Find Your Gaps

Identify existing assets

- Vendor lists and material requirements sheets
- Diagrams and schematics
- Checklists
- Formal training program
- No formal guidance
- OJT by word-of-mouth or personal demonstration

Drill Down into Target Area Methods

Methods and processes are the lubricant that run your business. Without good and documented methods and processes, your products and services would soon deteriorate and your business could flounder.

In some cases, the nature of your service for sale may be a method or process. This is especially true if you are a consulting firm. If that describes your business, you may spend most of your time in this arm of the Competitive Advantages Diagram.

Some Methods and Processes Can Be Easily Replicated

For most businesses, this exercise will focus on the methods and processes that run your business. Think about software applications that impose order on day-to-day operations. Your accounting software belongs here. So does your customer resource management (CRM) system. You probably use some kind of communication or team organizational software for scheduling meetings and directing work flow. That belongs here too. Most of these methods and processes are not critical because usually they can be purchased as software-as-a-service and many of the offerings in the market are somewhat interchangeable. If your method or process has been highly customized to meet a very specific business need, it is probably an essential asset. It can be replicated but with difficulty.

When a Method or Process Is Proprietary

For some businesses, the process or method is its intellectual property. In those cases, if you are selling your method or process, or your patented process is the secret sauce that produces your distinctive product, it belongs in the critical column. Some consultants sell patented or copyrighted systems for leadership programs, management methodologies, or personal growth pathways. Those things are methods and processes that are for sale. They are unique, and they are the lifeblood of the organization. If you happen to be in one of those businesses, you will probably spend most of your time in this area, and perhaps the man arm of the exercise as well, if a person or team is identified with executing and refining the method for customers.

Prioritize and Organize Your Information

Based on the above discussion, which methods or processes are nonessential, essential, or critical?

With your group, list your identified methods and processes into three categories on this chart. If you sell a process or methodology, as in the case of a consultancy, it belongs in the critical column. If your process is the secret sauce in producing your product, it also belongs in the critical column (Figure 4.7).

The Knowledge and Training Gap Exercise

After you have completed the Knowledge Stratification Exercise, figure out if you already have that knowledge captured and catalogued somewhere so it can be passed on.

First, transfer your essential and critical methods to the chart below. Then begin your search to fill out the columns to determine if you have a formal training program, some approved materials such as job aides, diagrams, or checklists to give to a new hire. For the majority of methods and processes that are nonproprietary and easily replicable, the instructions are enough.

For the cases where methods and processes are proprietary and therefore critical, you need to consider the associated legal, and possibly regulatory, information that is important to protect and maintain them as well as the steps or other intricate design elements of the process itself (Figure 4.8).

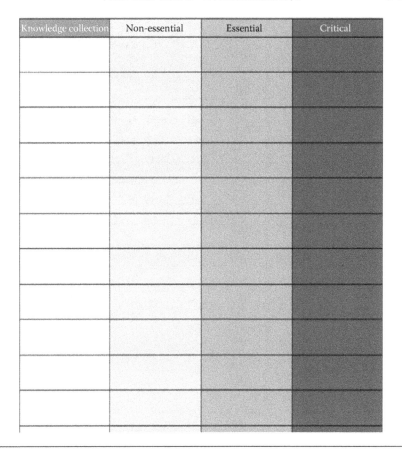

Knowledge collection	Non-essential	Essential	Critical

Figure 4.7   Organize and prioritize knowledge – method assets

Find Your Gaps

Identify existing assets

- Charts and graphs
- Diagrams and schematics
- Checklists
- Formal training program
- No formal guidance
- OJT by word-of-mouth or personal demonstration

Time and Resource Commitment

Depending on the size and complexity of your organization, you may complete the Competitive Advantage Chart, Identifying Your SMEs

Essential	Critical	No information; OJT	Job aids, diagrams, checklists	Formal training program

Figure 4.8   Identify training gaps – method assets

Functional Area and Role Chart, Knowledge Stratification Exercise and Knowledge and Training Gap Chart in one morning. However, if you have a medium-sized organization or a company that is dispersed in many locations, give yourself about a month or more to complete these exercises to account for the time you and your colleagues can dedicate to the process and to leave time to explore any revelations you had not anticipated.

If your organization is sizeable or complex, you will need to consider the fact that the expertise discovery phase of this project will consume considerable resources including the time of valuable people. However, because your organization is concerned about losing valuable information and people in the next few years, consider the commitment of resources an important investment in the future viability of your company.

I strongly recommend that if you commit to this process, that you also commit to completing the discovery phase of filling out the Competitive Advantages Diagram within a month. Any longer, and you will lose momentum, focus, and purpose. Besides, identifying your critical assets is only the beginning of what will become a continuous process of gathering, cataloguing, and updating information.

Next, you will begin to undertake the process of identifying and working with your internal subject matter experts. Expect that the process of identifying critical assets and gathering information from your subject matter experts will be an ongoing knowledge management process in your organization as part of your continuous quality improvement initiatives. After all, you will always develop and improve your products and services, and people who are new employees today are your subject matter experts of tomorrow – often in new products and services you have not developed or even imagined today. And if you plan to remain a viable enterprise into the future, expect that you will be developing products and services that are still only in the minds' eye of people you may not have even hired yet.

But for now, if you have conducted the above exercises, you have captured a snapshot of your enterprise as it exists today, and you know what you are looking for. Next, you will establish best practices for knowledge capture, preservation, and transfer.

It bears repeating. The rest of this process will be ongoing and is not time limited, so settle in for the long haul as you institute the ideas in the rest of this book.

After you have identified your geeks, gurus, and other irreplaceables and drilled down to determine what you must retain, it is time to establish a process to standardize information gathering or at least have a few best practices at your disposal to make the most of your knowledge collection efforts.

When you have irreplaceable knowledge, you cannot leave its capture, storage, and transfer to chance. This is a place where you can put a lot of effort into making sure that you have not only best practices for prioritizing and negotiating with your experts, but that you have the technology and tools in place to make the process as seamless as possible for the experts and the people who are tasked with capturing their expertise. When you choose tools and technology, consider your current capabilities but, more importantly, engage some of your best crystal ball IT people to help you select hardware, software, and platforms that will remain viable as technology changes. And it will.

Imagine going through the expensive process of identifying critical information for working with your subject matter experts only to find out a decade from now that the software and equipment you used to capture irreplaceable knowledge is no longer supported or can no longer be accessed. Your technology decisions are as important as any others at this stage of the game.

And with that in mind, let's proceed to Part 2 of this book and examine the tools and technology that will make your knowledge capture efforts efficient, pleasant, and worthwhile.

PART II

KNOWLEDGE MANAGEMENT IN THE AGE OF EXPONENTIAL TECHNOLOGICAL ADVANCES

5

COLLECTION, STORAGE, AND DELIVERY CHALLENGES FOR CAPTURING EXPERTISE

It was a hot Saturday afternoon in August 2016, and I had just returned from a strategy session with our local Association for Talent Development chapter. There was a lot of experience, knowledge, and skill in the room on the verge of retiring, or recently retired, from different careers in the talent development field. We were trying to decide how to continue to grow our local chapter to meet the needs of a new generation facing new challenges and employing different learning styles while having great technology at their fingertips.

We agreed. We have to reach out to the Millennials. Our mantra: We need more Millennials in the chapter.

It was clear that we were talking amongst ourselves because so few younger people were in the room. Millennials are rarely at these pedantic, live meetings. They are at home, or out and about online, getting their social interaction and information from their smartphones quickly and concisely, having several interactions simultaneously.

A year later I ran into the chapter president, and she had retired from her job as the head of training for a global brand 3 months earlier. I inquired how she was enjoying retirement, and she told me about the music and photography interests she is able to pursue. Then, she shocked me when she said she still had not stepped down as chapter president because she was in the midst of her second consecutive term with no promise of a successor. She discussed possibly pulling another past president out of retirement. But, as I see it, we face a much more serious issue, and that is generations learn and relate differently. Another nearby chapter president in an area bustling with global corporate and top drawer academic activity told me the same story in the past few months – sparsely attended meetings and difficulty finding local leadership. This is not a criticism of ATD at all. The organization has undergone much change in response to its constituency. However, as a past chapter president and board member for nearly a decade, I note that the change in our relating and learning styles is hitting our local ATD chapters in the same way it is hitting the workplace. In the intervening 12 months since that summer meeting, I am seeing signs that the older generation is either letting go or having control wrest from them by an enthusiastic young cohort grabbing the reins and redirecting the entire field of training and development. It is exhilarating to watch unfold.

The same conundrums we face in the local ATD chapter are happening in the workplace. The generations have different frames of reference, and those differences can manifest as an inability to understand or communicate with each other. The differences also express themselves in the way we meet in real time over lunch, or in a 20 minute Skype session. As Millennials take charge, these changes are accelerating.

No matter which generational cohort you associate with, if you feel like you are having trouble transferring generational learning among colleagues, ask yourself:

- Are we talking past each other?
- Do we respect each other as individuals?
- Is there a parent-child dynamic going on?
- Do we respect each other's knowledge and skills?
- Do we understand each other's attitudes?
- Are we using the right communication vehicles?

The ultimate question then is, "How do we transfer knowledge among generations where these issues exist?" And they often do.

At this point in history, it is clear that effective knowledge transfer is not just a matter of integrating technology or understanding different learning styles. If you are facing obstructions in your efforts to collect and transfer knowledge in your corporation, perhaps there are deeper issues to be explored. In a book on transferring knowledge from retiring workers to the next generation of workers, it is worthwhile to spend time addressing potential interpersonal and intergenerational hurdles.

Sometimes, the mere act of acknowledging an issue takes you most of the way toward solving it. In that spirit, let us look at the human side of learning transfer among the generations.

Learning Transfer with the Multigenerational Workforce

Recently, I worked inside a company where nearly everyone was younger than me, some people by decades. I learned firsthand the daily sensitivities of a multigenerational workforce which are very different than my usual experience of the occasional, visiting consultant.

There are still a lot of us Baby Boomers, but now there are more Next Gen Workers.

Baby boomers are accustomed to being the largest generation. However, as of April 2016, officially and statistically, Millennials outnumber Boomers.[*] The reason for this is, well, only the luckiest of the Boomers are not getting any younger.

As the "Me Generation" and one that is living healthier in a world of medical advances, Boomers are sticking around the workplace longer, giving up control later and more reluctantly, and some – like me – do not plan on retiring at all. If you do what you love, why stop?

But here are some of the economic realities underpinning the Boomers' long stay in the workforce.

When Medicare was passed in 1965, the actuarial projections showed that the average senior would live less than 10 years past retirement for the purposes of the analysis.[†] That is one of the many reasons Medicare and Social Security are in such dire financial straits today. People live a lot longer than originally anticipated when those social safety nets were strung together. Subsequently, seniors use a lot more resources than the program was built to absorb. With more grey heads and wrinkles hanging around the office, it is harder to pass authority to the next generation when institutional knowledge is sitting next to you.

---

[*] Accessed September 26, 2017 at http://www.pewresearch.org/fact-tank/2016/04/25/millennials-overtake-baby-boomers/.

[†] Accessed September 26, 2017 at http://www.indexmundi.com/facts/united-states/life-expectancy-at-birth.

The reality, though, is that for some Boomers it is fun to turn the power and authority over to the next generation and just hang out and make a contribution without the need to get ahead any longer. But this dynamic causes tension because - more today than ever before - it is common for young people to lead teams that include elders. And who wants to lead a team with your father reporting to you...or worse, your mother?

Conversely, some elders look down on their younger coworkers. Who wants their kids telling them what to do?

This tug creates interpersonal tension. However, managed well, intergenerational teams can bring a lot of power to an organization. Let us look at some of the generational interplay and how to manage it.

Mutual Respect and Low Threat Interactions

At this point, let us explore the way that intergenerational tensions can affect learning transfer.

Entitlement

Dan Rockwell of Leadership Freak writes in an August 2016 blog,[*] "Entitlement expects respect or opportunity without earning it. Elders may expect respect simply because they've been at it longer. Youngers may expect opportunity or position simply because they want it... Both elders and youngers may feel the other doesn't get it."

Bearing that in mind, let us look at ways to handle the tension that entitlement brings to the workplace.

For the Older Gen

Think back to the time when you were 25 or 35 and you were raising a young family and building your career. You were pretty bright. Well, so are the intelligent, driven, experienced members of the leadership team in your organization who are younger than you. Respect them. They have earned it through 10 or 15 years in the trenches and you have a lot to learn from them. Their experiences are different, they

---

[*] Accessed September 26, 2017 at https://leadershipfreak.wordpress.com/2016/08/14/7-ways-young-leaders-succeed-with-elders/.

are making deals with their peers (who often do not want to make deals with you, by the way), and they are building your company to meet the future. They have experiences and frames of reference that are relevant for driving the business in the direction it needs to go today. Be willing to be part of the team and a contributing member. Have a learner's mindset. Contribute from your experience but respect your team members and their leadership. They have earned it and they deserve it. If they want your advice or guidance, they can ask for it. Make it easy for them to do that by showing you admire and respect them. If you treat them like kids, you deserve to be treated like an old fart.

For the Younger Gen

You might feel like you are working with your mother and deep down inside, you may resent it. Subconsciously, it feels like she will tell you to eat your veggies and wipe your nose. She will not. Remember when your mom left the house with her briefcase in the morning and came home at night, kicked off her heels, and fell into the lounge chair with a big sigh? She was out all day, doing what you are doing. She was not making peanut butter and jelly sandwiches at work. She was planning strategy, building businesses, making deals, directing the course of events that you are part of today. You can ask older workers for some perspective. You might be surprised that the old lady or old man sitting there actually knows a thing or two that is relevant to what you are doing. Some knowledge and skills are timeless, and most attitudes are. Take advantage of what the grey head might know. That old woman who looks like your mother does not care if you eat your veggies. She really does not. But she does care about the future of your business; that is why she is sitting there. And she might have a few nuggets of insight about your company and industry for all her years in the field.

Young Workers Have the Greater Challenge

According to Rockwell's Leadership Freak blog *7 Ways Young Leaders Succeed with Elders*, the greater challenge of working on intergenerational teams lies with the younger people. In order to thrive, young leaders must navigate elders who have more experience, power, resources, and prestige.

Dan Rockwell's 7 Ways Young Leaders Succeed with Elders

#1. Show respect, even if you don't feel respected. It is self-defeating to expect respect before extending it.

Honor knowledge, even if you feel smarter. Ask questions. Stay curious.

Honor experience, even if you feel it is no big deal. Invite and listen to stories.

Honor position, even if hierarchy irritates you. Learn how they earned their positions.

Connection with elders is forged with respect.

Showing respect is about a humble heart. When you feel misunderstood, remember to understand others.

#2. Adopt a learner's attitude. Older leaders often feel superior because they believe they are more knowledgeable. You may know more than your elders, but you have not experienced more.

Elders feel disrespected when youngers offhandedly reject suggestions.

#3. Build a team of elder advisors. *Make it public that you are listening to mentors.* Publicly talk about things you are learning from elders.

#4. Try on suggestions that rub you the wrong way. I have found that wisdom often seems wrong when I am unenlightened. I am still rejecting ideas that make sense later.

#5. Find an elder advocate who believes and supports you. Some elders value the perspective and talent of young leaders.

#6. Focus on adding value more than receiving it. How might you help elders achieve their goals?

#7. Work hard.

A special thank you to Dan Rockwell for permission to include his thinking here.

Intergenerational Challenges Affect Learning Transfer

When younger colleagues do not feel respected, it is hard for them to learn from older team members. Younger members could be defensive

("You think you know so much?") or threatened ("You will make me look stupid.").

Either of these attitudes affect knowledge transfer. It is hard, if not impossible, to hear someone when you feel defensive or threatened. Yet, most likely, older workers have valuable knowledge to be transferred, and they also have historical context either about the company or the industry that could help you solve problems you have right now. Historical knowledge or context could help younger leaders get to the heart of the matter much faster by taking short cuts, avoiding mistakes, or seeing things from a different perspective.

Older workers can help younger workers learn from them by avoiding an attitude of superiority or "know-it-all-ness." Nobody wants to feel stupid or inferior. Let your younger leaders know that you support their growth and respect their contributions. Make it safe for them to turn to you for advice and help. Also, make it clear you do not plan on hanging around forever and would like to be able to make contributions that will allow the company to succeed and excel long after you have your toes in the sand in Florida.

Technological Comfort Zone

One common misconception is that older workers are not comfortable with technology. Older workers may be very comfortable with technology and use it to its best advantage. They may not, however, be as facile with technological tips and tricks that younger workers understand intuitively.

This is true for learning software, too. Building training programs in e-learning software has changed from stone age complexity to what-you-see-is-what-you-get (WYSIWYG) simplicity in just a decade. So make sure that your technology is the latest, and that all members of the team are trained on it appropriately. Ideally, your experienced subject matter experts will become besties with an iPad and will be able to upload their knowledge using video, audio, and their documents to make it available to people who need it.

The danger is that when subject matter experts are set loose with a video program and can create their own training snippets, their contributions will not be properly captured, catalogued. and made available within the learning resource system at your company. If you set a SME loose with the ability to create his or her own training, make sure the training department is managing the process from the selection of the material to be captured to the means to capture it to the way it will be stored and filed for easy retrieval later.

This process is best done in collaboration with the expert and knowledge management team because they will be able to determine how certain types of information are most successfully transferred. When choosing the best technology to transfer information, ask questions like:

- Would it be more accessible and easier to understand if that information was simply captured on a physical job aide that hangs at a workstation?
- Is this process one that needs to be seen in action and explained verbally, and therefore, would benefit from creating a short video?
- Would that concept be best explained in a diagram within a slide presentation that breaks down its component parts slide by slide with an audio explanation?

Those decisions are best made by the training experts in cooperation with the SME. It is helpful to keep in mind that your goal is to categorize and simplify sometimes complex knowledge. Experts know so much, so deeply, they wonder – and you may wonder – how could they ever explain it to you. Actually, your experts not only can explain it but when you guide them systematically, they can drop bread crumbs all along the learning path for you in a way that makes it easy to follow.

As training specialists, instructional designers, or any other content developer tasked with capturing expertise, you are in a position to create a logical and easy to understand learning path. Some experts are hard wired to think sequentially and teach what they know, but others are not and that is where the guidance of a content developer is most valuable.

In the beginning of your knowledge capture adventure with an expert, get a feel for the whole body of knowledge that you are wrangling with. Lay out what you think is a logical path and check with your expert. When you both agree on the parameters of the topic, create milestones, subcategories, or some other measures that break up the material into easily digestible bites.

After you have agreed on the full scope of work and its subcomponents, create a common language – or tag – for each part based on symbols, numbers, words or some other descriptors that allows both you and the learner to have a frame of reference for the sequence and internal relationship of the material to the whole. The tags create stationary markers or a taxonomy to guide you.

When you and your expert have agreed upon the general scope of the content, create content tags in cooperation with the expert to categorize the material. These tags, determined early in the process, give you both a way to know where something belongs as you collect information from your expert. Tags help organize material in the software tool or method you choose to capture the information. It will also help you figure out what is most important and what kinds of information are secondary "nice to knows." See the diagram in Part III for an explanation about how to sort main ideas from secondary ones.

Often your expert will think something is more important than you do. Your expert may insist certain things be included that will make the curriculum or your other content too long or too complicated for the level of learning expected. Your tags help you categorize and create a hierarchy for what is most essential to stay on the direct learning path.

You can always take secondary or non-essential information and add it to an appendix, glossary, or popup. When you have created a learning path, it will help you both remain clear on what is most important and what information is supplementary or can wait for the next level of information that you develop.

When you have chosen the best method and a plan for capture, make sure your SME is comfortable with the software solution that you are using. A little patience goes a long way in training anyone on new technology, especially a generation for whom some operations and screens are not intuitive. Embed your learning path and the tags you have created so your expert has guidance built into your collection tool as he or she works to deliver knowledge.

Millennials grew up knowing what happens when they right click and which option leads to which screen. Boomers may have built much of what the world uses today, but that technology was developed by a small cohort. For the next few years, companies may have to accept that some of the greyest of the grey heads are still using AOL to get email. Some battles are not worth fighting. The goal is to capture their areas of expertise, not help them develop new ones. Your older workers have made the bulk of their contributions and want to pass it on. Make it easy for the least technologically facile among them to do so. Consider it part of the job of capturing their expertise.

Age-Related Illnesses and Biological Changes

I have actually incurred some criticism for the following advice, saying it is "age-ist" or that it presumes disability accompanies age. To set the record straight, I do not assume disability accompanies age, but I also recognize that some biological changes are common, and when you work with retiring or aging workers, there are issues you may face. With that disclaimer, let us discuss the topic of age-related illnesses and biological changes.

When your experts are approaching retirement, you will probably have to accommodate some age-related biological changes as you work with them. Not all older workers will be ill or have age-related limitations, but some will.

You may have to account for the following as you work with older subject matter experts:

- Hearing and eyesight deteriorate over time in many people.
- Your expert may get tired before you do.
- Some older workers retire for health reasons, so be ready to accommodate their ability to navigate steps or even make it into the office to work with you. Consider off-site meetings if necessary.
- Your expert may be on a medication schedule.
- Your expert may have a serious illness such as cancer, and you will need to work around treatments and doctor appointments. Some days will be better than others for them.

It is possible that your younger workers exhibit some of these health-related issues as well, but it is more likely that you will run into them with older workers, including your expert. Having had the honor of working with some very distinguished octogenarians, I feel that it is important to mention here that you may encounter these issues and you will want to be prepared with some tactics for overcoming situations that may present barriers to knowledge transfer. Work with your expert to determine any special accommodations or considerations they may need to make the process comfortable for them.

Peaceful Coexistence

As your company works through the interpersonal and technological challenges presented by intergenerational knowledge transfer, keep in mind that this process can occur in an atmosphere of peaceful coexistence. Peaceful coexistence is best achieved by mutual respect and a mutual desire to ensure that your company succeeds in the marketplace in the short and long run.

After all, chances are that some of your experts contributed in a great way to the fact that your company exists and thrives today. They have an interest in their work lasting beyond their involvement in it. They appreciate your advice, experience, and interest in making sure their work survives them more than you might think.

6

CREATING A TECH PLAN
FOR CAPTURING EXPERTISE

The kind of information you need to capture will dictate how to collect it, how to store it, and how to pass it on. The technology, tools, and methods you choose to use for those tasks will also impact the process. As you select technology to capture knowledge and pass it on, you will also need to consider who will be using the tools to make sure that the technology and approach:

a. Are comfortable for the subject matter expert,
b. Are the best ways to collect the kind of information that you are gathering,
c. Lend themselves to the storage capabilities and methods available within your organization, and
d. Will facilitate the way that learners will want to learn the subject.

Step One: Determine the Kind of Information You Are Collecting

When you are creating a plan for working with your SME, you need to consider the kind of information you will be collecting. You want to make sure that you are gathering information in a way that makes it easy to put into the best format for transferring it to learners later. You will be gathering information from experts as diverse as machine operators, accountants, software engineers, warehouse floor supervisors, and corporate executives. Each task and each type of expert require different handling as well as different tools to capture their expertise.

For example, if you are collecting information about proprietary business software, it is best to be able to capture the program using a training application that allows the learner to imitate operations in a simulation. To save time and steps later, this is where a training professional has value because an expert in your software application, for example, may skip steps that are intuitive to him as he describes data inputs and operations. A trainer's eye will be sure that all the steps are captured sequentially and that nothing is missed. For example, a training professional will think to look at all the drop down boxes and see what is hiding in them; whereas, a software expert may gloss over what he considers to be obvious steps such as "click next to proceed."

Alternately, if you are discussing the details of your sales model, you may want to record audio discussions, collect slide presentations, and even accompany crack sales people on their calls to capture the subtleties that you will not gather in a discussion.

The variety of experts and their areas of expertise require a training professional to oversee knowledge capture. While subject matter experts are very smart at what they do, they will not all intuitively know how to teach what they do. In fact, the very nature of expertise often means that they are unconscious competents, that is, experts who perform tasks unconsciously because they have been doing their jobs for so long that they no longer have to think about them in a stepwise fashion. A training professional is there to ensure that no steps are missed, and knowledge is captured in a way that is comprehensible to the naïve learner.

Finally, even if you decide that the best method for collecting information from experts is to record them, they may not like to be captured on video. You will need to adjust your collection methods to the preferences of your experts, so they are most comfortable and open to sharing what they know.

Step Two: Collect Knowledge in Formats That Complement It

This step grows organically out of the last one. Since you have done a thorough search for experts in every corner of your organization, you will be talking to machine operators, biochemical scientists, lawyers, corporate executives, sales staff, and accountants to name only a few. Their knowledge will be in their heads, but bits and pieces will also be available in other formats.

The core of knowledge collection is the personal interview. Whenever possible, you need to meet and talk with your subject matter experts. You will get invaluable nuggets from those interviews and even learn the names of other experts you may not have discovered in the Functional Roles and Areas Mapping Exercise. So while the interview is the first and most important collection tool at your disposal, there are a lot of other ways you can and should capture and collect expertise.

As I mentioned earlier, if you are capturing a software developer's intricate knowledge about the operations related to a critical piece of software, it is best to capture him performing all the steps and recording the operations. That type of recording of the critical asset may be accompanied by detailed relevant information stored in a pdf document. If you are the one overseeing the knowledge capture event, you will know what you are looking for to determine if you have all the related relevant information stored in ways that make the entire knowledge capture complete.

Here are some considerations as you decide the best collection method for your expert's knowledge.

Audio and video capture of the interview: Make an audio or video recording of almost all experts as they explain what they do. If you are speaking to a machine operator, capture a video of her performing her job. If you are discussing corporate policy with an executive, get an audio recording of your discussion.

Notetaking: Write down what experts tell you. Have them check details for accuracy. Even if you are getting audio or video recordings, you still need to take notes. Sometimes the recordings fail or are unintelligible in spots, and you will need your notes to reconstruct your interview. Sometimes an expert gives you the best nuggets after you have ended the recording and you are walking out the door. Also, good notetaking will include the time, date, and location of the interview, the correct spelling of interviewee's name and title, contact information, the next scheduled interview, and availability. This is all information that you may not have on a recording. Notetaking can include sketching ideas, concepts, processes, and similar content that lend themselves to diagrams or charts. See the interview checklist in Part III for details on how to conduct a thorough interview.

Slide presentations and speeches: Collect and store any critical information that your experts have delivered in public in the form of their slide presentations, speakers' notes, and speeches. Ask them if they have created these kinds of resources.

Diagrams, lists, and charts: Collect and store any schematics, diagrams, checklists, charts, infographics, or any other internal materials that capture a process, describe a machine. or explain data. While most of these types of materials are stored electronically, do not overlook old schematics taped to the side of a machine or blueprints stored in a drawer for example.

White papers, journal articles, and books: Your expert may be an externally recognized authority in the field and have published documents in peer reviewed journals, written college textbooks, or have had articles published in professional periodicals both online and in hard copy. I recommend you collect these as well in the spirit that your expert, by definition, is an unconscious competent and has forgotten to tell you half or more of what he or she knows. In some cases, that unarticulated expertise that will help you connect the dots is out there somewhere.

Step Three: Store and Translate the Information into Learning Materials

For all your collection efforts to pay off, store and create materials that allow for clear transfer of the information to learners later. If you have chosen your collection method to best complement the type of expertise you are gathering, your job should be at least halfway complete. In some cases, such as the case of capturing screen shots from a software expert explaining how to execute operations, it may be mostly complete.

The types of materials you have collected will dictate how you store and translate them into learning materials. Since the point of expert material is that it will be initially incomprehensible to nonexperts, your job will be to apply good instructional design principles to the materials. This is not a discussion on instructional design; however, suffice it to say that a training professional will be able to make sure the material is made available in a stepwise fashion governed by sound instructional principles. Some educational software is designed with many of the elements of good instructional design built in. For our purposes here, after you have collected information from your subject matter expert, your task will be to make sure that you save it in a way that is organized, can be easily retrieved, and can be understood by others.

When you are gathering particularly difficult or complex material, you will probably have to build a learning program from the ground up to teach foundational principles and guide the learner toward acquiring sophisticated information.

However, for the purposes of storage and retrieval, if you have gathered white papers and blueprints from your experts, your main task will be to make sure they are stored so they will not degrade and are organized so they can be easily found by people who need them. This applies to both electronic and physical documents.

Again, you know by the types of material you have collected and the resources you have at your disposal how best to store and communicate them to the next generation of learners. No matter your circumstance, make sure the materials are stored in a way that they can be preserved, retrieved and understood later.

What Kinds of Expertise Can You Capture? All Kinds!

Up until now, you have heard me reference knowledge, skills, and attitudes of your experts – the KSAs. This is a good time to review exactly what kinds of expertise you can capture. As I mentioned earlier, when you are thinking about your competitive advantages, you are looking not only for specific information or skill sets, but you are also looking for attitudes that are worth preserving in order to continue the corporate culture.

The answer to the kinds of expertise can you capture is: Everything.

You can capture everything, but admittedly, some things are much harder to bottle than others. I mentioned earlier the story of John, the irreplaceable biochemical engineer. John was not only an expert in the company's products, processes, and history, but he also embodied the corporate culture by his style of relating, the way he dressed, and his attitude toward his work. He was respectful but not obsequious. He dressed neatly but not formally. He had a passion for what he did, and it was infectious. He was a *bona fide* genius but humble and humorous. Was this transferrable? Absolutely! But in this case, the best transfer of his attitude required other employees' interactions with him. As he deported himself and communicated with others, he set an example that others admired and wanted to follow.

All kinds of expertise can be captured. It is up to you to decide the best method for doing that.

About KSAs

When you are looking for critical information from your internal subject matter experts, you will find it in all three domains: knowledge, skills, and attitudes. And to pull out John as an example one more time, you may find all three in one individual. Can you successfully capture and transfer all three? Absolutely! This is where the creativity of an instructional designer comes in. The answers to how best to capture and transfer the knowledge, skills, and attitudes that are necessary to preserve your company's critical competitive advantages are the core of all sound instructional design.

The following is a very brief highlight of what you are looking for when you are searching for your critical KSAs, how best to capture them, and some of the most effective ways to teach them. This is by no means comprehensive or even always true (make room for exceptions and creativity). But for people who are concerned about preserving your internal expertise, this serves as a brief primer so you can understand some of the theory and best practices you will need to most effectively oversee the work of transferring the best that your subject matter experts have to offer.

Knowledge – what they *know*, what is in their heads

Skills – what they can *do*, which can include a machine operator but also a talented people manager or negotiator

Attitudes – the *way* they work, their styles and approaches to the company and profession

About Knowledge

What is knowledge? What is in their heads.

How do you capture it? Get them to talk, record them, collect the artifacts of their work such as papers, slide presentations, and articles.

How do you teach it? This often lends itself best to live classroom, but well-presented webinars and e-learning programs can accomplish the same goals. Provide written materials, charts, graphs, and so on.

About Skills

What are skills? What they do with their hands.

How do you capture them? Video recording, demonstrations, schematics, steps and directions with photographs and drawings.

How do you teach them? See one, do one. Hands-on practice. Role plays.

About Attitudes

What are attitudes? Their styles and approaches, the ways they feel, and the ways they make others feel.

How do you capture them? Personal interaction is the best teacher.

How do you teach them? Exposure to those who embody the corporate culture, mentoring programs, reinforcement with inspirational posters, audio and video reminders, checklists, and visual prompts such as signs in meeting rooms.

After you have identified the types of information that you need to capture and the best methods for doing so, it is time to look at the options available for capture, storage, and transfer of your critical expertise.

7

THE BENEFITS OF
TERRIFIC TECHNOLOGY

Ah, herein lies temptation. My first instinct was to spend this chapter solely discussing training technology. Several software companies are dedicating themselves to creating the most user-friendly knowledge capture tools so that subject matter experts can go straight to putting their masterful content into a training program and cut out the pesky middleman, the instructional designer.

But while I will indulge my desire to discuss some terrific tech tools that are on the market to make instructional design easy for subject matter experts, this section is also a good place to mention a few limiting factors you need to consider when looking at the ideal technology for capturing, storing, and delivering content. After you have considered these issues, then we will go forth to bring on some of the very best tech tools the world has to offer.

Briefly, here are some constraints that must be considered in your quest for the perfect tech tool.

1. Technology changes. Make sure you are capturing knowledge in a way that you can retrieve it later. Remember "3-inch floppies"? I did not think so.
2. Learning styles change. Yesterday's 3-hour computer-based e-learning program is today's 2-minute video clip.
3. Choose solutions that support your learners. Subject matter experts are brilliant biochemical engineers. They are not instructional designers who, yes, have to go to school for that.

With those caveats, let us dig into a discussion of your options for capturing, warehousing. and delivering the knowledge, skills, and attitudes currently housed in your experts' brains.

Before You Buy, Remember: Technology Changes

The promise of technology is so fabulous that when you are thinking about how to work with your subject matter expert, it is tempting to go straight to the sexiest new tool. And for a lot of knowledge capture, quite frankly, that is your best option. Before looking at your software and hardware options, however, you need to decide if that pricey new program is the best route for accomplishing your goals.

I may be booed off the planet for this statement, but let me suggest that not every problem has a software solution.

Consider the following before making an investment in software and, quite possibly, hardware, to put into the hands of your instructional designers or directly into the hands of your experts. The answers to these questions will influence your choices of collection, storage, and delivery methods.

1. What is the shelf life of this knowledge? Is this the kind of information you want to preserve for posterity or is this something that you expect to need only for the next quarter or the next year?
2. Who will be using the software or hardware? Instructional designers with video and audio editing sophistication or writers with limited WYSIWG skills? Or will subject matter experts themselves be uploading content, writing test questions and learning objectives, and be expected to create the training program with little or no oversight from instructional designers?
3. Are you purchasing software or some other tech tool that must be compatible with current programs and a legacy learning management system (LMS)?
4. Are you moving away from legacy e-learning software and LMS infrastructure? If so, have you thoroughly mapped out the future of your learning strategies so your purchases support your longer-term investments?
5. Is a tech tool, even something as simple as a slide presentation, the right way to present this information? Does this knowledge capture need to be a white paper? A diagram on a physical chart hanging in a workstation? A speech with a handout? A physical blueprint or schematic? A hands-on demonstration of a tool or process? A job shadow or mentoring

experience? Think about what you are trying to capture, retain, and deliver and what kind of vehicle best supports the transfer of expertise from expert to novice.

After you have answered these questions, and you still decide that you need new hardware and software to accomplish learning transfer in the most efficient way, then yes, crack open your checkbook and buy what you need to do the job right.

Learning Styles Change

This subject deserves a book of its own, and in fact, many of those books have already been written. Suffice it to say here that Baby Boomers got most of their educations by reading books – very, very long and heavy books –about a lot of heavy topics. They spent interminable hours in the stacks at the university library, dusting off old tomes and scouring tables of contents in the front and thousands of index items in the back of those hard-backed storehouses of knowledge, looking for just one precious nugget of information. I am one of those dinosaurs, so I remember it well. That means Baby Boomers did not mind sitting through a 3-hour e-learning program in 2001. Heck, spending a single afternoon learning something new in front of a cathode ray tube was a breeze!

At the risk of belaboring the obvious, let us reinforce here that Boomers' children and grandchildren learn in little snippets. They ask Siri™. They Google™ it. Massive amounts of pertinent and current information are in our pockets now. These are the learners for whom you are capturing, storing, and delivering content. So, you need to be creating bits of important just-in-time learning that are easy to access, digest, and assimilate into the work environment.

When you are capturing true expertise for preservation, you need to consider not only how people learn today, but also how they may learn tomorrow. With the pace of change, it truly is speculative at this point in human history. You do not know if virtual reality (VR) will become common in the workplace, a la Pokemon Go™ or Google Glass™, but the smart money says it will. The implications of VR for learning by doing are limited only by your imagination. Medical students will not have to practice surgery – or even just patient interactions – on real patients, for example. One trainer and expert in neurolinguistic programming (NLP)*, Mike Hoffmeister, explained the potential of working with his clients in Holland using VR to help them overcome fears like fear of flying and agoraphobia.

If, indeed, VR is the future of learning that may influence how you choose to capture knowledge today. You need to take a lot of video to be able to recreate an experience when your expert has long ago left town for a condo in Arizona and VR becomes the go-to learning technology at your company. Get video that captures his motions from all angles, his expressions, his intricate hand gestures because that will help you recreate the virtual expert later.

You cannot predict the pace of the uptake of something like VR or its potential uses. You must, however, consider currently available technology when you are thinking about how people will learn a skill in the future. Imagine the possibilities of role plays for sales professionals if you can put a "real" holographic customer in front of them at their desks to practice their selling skills while having to think on their feet. Using avatars in a virtual reality game such as the Second Life™ experience was only the early edge of the potential of this kind of technology. What about a management course on how to correct a holographic employee? How about being part of a holographic dance team practicing a synchronized routine? Think about your own company in light of these examples, and how VR could accelerate the learning process in some of those real time, you've-gotta-do-it-to-get-it types of skills.

With that in mind, take into account the different kinds of knowledge you need to retain from your experts and how best to capture them to be able to feed that into the learning systems you use now as well as the ones you could be able to build tomorrow.

Real time, just in time, and on demand – these are where real learning is happening and these trends are not likely to revert to slow, plodding learning styles. Deep learning takes time, and there will always be a place – or so I believe at this point in history anyway – for weighty, 800-page graduate level books and long lectures from grey heads in stadium seating lecture halls in the red brick or gray cement buildings of academia. Maybe it is my sentimental attachment to the accoutrements of traditional higher education that feed the conceit that there

---

* A very crude definition of neurolinguistic programming (NLP) is that NLP studies the way language shapes our belief systems and actions.

will always be a purpose for learning in that way. Having said that, we know from experience that is not where most learning happens today. It is not even preferable that most learning happen there today.

Real learning is about delivering content in a way that the student can absorb it, relate to it, and immediately execute it. This approach is even more crucial when you are creating and delivering content for adult learners. Adult learners build on what they already know. They do more of what they have done. And that goes not just for content but also for the learning style and approach.

Now that learners are accustomed to speed and accessibility, consider that most of your content needs to be readily available and consumable in small bites. Whenever appropriate, choose collection, storage, and delivery methods that support just in time learning.

Technology – The Story That AI Built

At least one company is playing with using artificial intelligence to take photos and other electronic artifacts to build a story by interpreting them. Then real humans check the story that AI built to see how closely it mirrors the reality associated with the electronic inputs.

This technology has promise for building training from limited assets when no other information is available. If this technology proves that it can build a realistic story from historical assets, it has possible application to the training world if experts are lost, but some electronic remnants – such as photos – remain of the original knowledge.

While it is highly exploratory right now, AI might be part of the answer to lost knowledge. Just as we are getting close to reconstructing extinct species using fragments of DNA (cue Jurassic Park), we may be able to reconstruct knowledge from limited pictorial evidence. Just maybe.

The point is that we do not know exactly where technology takes us, but we can be sure it will be somewhere that we have never been.

Here's a Zen mind trick: Consider the unimaginable when you imagine the future of learning.

Technology – Ease of Use, Storage, and Transfer

If you have filtered your training needs through the technology assessment questions presented at the beginning of this chapter and have decided that you need to purchase a software solution, choose something that supports your SMEs on the front end and your learners on the back end.

Having spent a significant part of my career as a content developer and instructional designer working with subject matter experts, I can say with some confidence that one of the greatest challenges your training designer faces is making sure they are capturing the most relevant information from an expert in a field about which your training designer knows almost nothing. The next challenge is to present it in a way that neophytes can absorb it. Instructional designers (IDs) have skills sets that support safe transfer of knowledge and expertise to meet these criteria.

Instructional designers have an important role with subject matter experts. If you remove the learning professional from the transfer of expertise, you risk losing material transfer to poor instructional execution. Therefore, while there is a movement afoot to put knowledge capture tools directly into the hands of subject matter experts, it is important that experts have guidance and the process is well thought out and directed by professional trainers and instructional designers.

Here are a few of the tech tools available today to meet these needs easily.

Many subject matter experts are naturally gifted storytellers; there is one web-based software, called Knovio®, that gives them the platform to share their knowledge, passion, and authority with ease using video, audio, and slide presentations. With advanced syncing capabilities and powerful interactive player options, experts can create the perfect viewing experience that includes video or audio, notations, transcripts, chapters, quizzes, and much more. Knovio also provides all the feature functionality of a video platform, so users can host, share, and analyze all these presentations and videos too. The Knovio Online Video Platform was developed by KnowledgeVision®, a pioneer in delivering powerful video technology solutions that are easy to use and remarkably affordable.

Other challenges await you if you would like your experts to capture structured information and build an instructionally sound training program on their own using e-learning software programs.

Software designers have addressed that issue by building programs that prepopulate learning objectives so they are written correctly and use an "insert object here" strategy that directs the SME to input the correct information in the best format in the right place. New startup Synapse® offers a software program that builds in the instructional design elements allowing a SME to work in the program and create a well-structured training program left pretty much on his or her own by following prompts.

> Synapse enables companies to share knowledge from internal experts, top performers, and leaders with employees and customers. Anyone in a company can build engaging digital training in less time than creating a PowerPoint™.

> **Ryan Austin, CEO** [*]

Other instructional software allows trainers to create just in time snippets for "preinforcement," new microlearning, and reinforcement. One company, count5[†], developed software q.MINDshare™ that supports experts in writing and delivering questions, tips, videos, and other bite sized content on a scheduled, regular basis to learners' computers and mobile devices where learners can respond and interact. The program records interactions and answers so learner responses can be tracked and assessed. q.MINDshare remembers each user's learning gaps and schedules additional reinforcement to close them. count5™ offers courses on assessment design and microlearning best practices tailored for experts, so customers get better outcomes from their training investment.

> Companies don't pay learning & development to deliver training; they pay them to deliver business outcomes. The "forgetting curve" is real – without reinforcement, users forget more than half their training. count5 has developed a process and technology that interrupts the forgetting curve, driving faster and more predictable outcomes.

> **Eric G. Blumthal, CEO, count5**

Other software programs on the market perform similar or complementary functions. You will know what works best in your situation as

---

[*] From Ryan Austin, September 7, 2017 per email.
[†] In full disclosure, I have worked for and with some of these companies, so I know their products, what they can do, and the knowledge transfer needs they fill.

you review the options available at the time you are looking for solutions for your company. These programs are all different but all have value in giving subject matter experts more direct input and control over the final learning product. More options with user-friendly features are entering the market all the time so your search will uncover options not available as of this writing.

Thinking Much Longer Term

For most of your needs, the solutions available today will safely capture, store, and transfer knowledge from your experts to learners outside their spheres of influence, beyond their tenure with your company, and most likely even after their lifetimes.

A much trickier problem deserves at least a passing mention in this book. You may want some expertise to survive long after your grandchildren have joined you in the great beyond. Much of the knowledge we are accumulating today has lasting value and long-term ramifications for the survival and progress of the human species. Your company may have products and processes that should be preserved for millennia. And yes, people work on problems like that too.

If you are reading this book, you are probably looking for a short-term practical solution to an immediate problem, so I will not spend too much time on this topic. But it is worth mentioning that it helps to be aware that some of what your company is doing may have long-term implications for the human race. Only you know that. But if it does, your methods of storage and the ability to retrieve such information at a far distant date are affected by your decisions today.

A professor emeritus of physics at the University of California, Irvine Gregory Benford wrote a fascinating nonfiction book, *Deep Time: How Humanity Communicates Across Millenia.* It chronicles his work with the U.S. Department of Energy in which he was part of an elite team tasked with figuring out how to find ways to dispose of dangerous materials in a way that reduces their chances of being uncovered or misused in a future when some hapless human or other creature could stumble upon them and accidentally unleash its threats. *Deep Time* is not science fiction, although it reads like it is, because Benford is best known for his work in the genre.

Benford and associates wrangled with problems about the preservation of knowledge and protection of artifacts through geopolitical upheaval, geographic dislocations, and radical climatic changes. He discusses these issues with some of the best minds on the planet. How might language and humans change and evolve over millennia? What are the chances anyone will be left who speaks English? What are the chances anyone will even be left? What are the chances we will still have two arms, two legs, ten fingers and toes, two eyes, and one brain wired to receive and interpret information the way we do today? What are the chances that an indigenous human will even be the intelligent life that stumbles upon this knowledge or artifact? All interesting yet esoteric questions.

For your limited purposes on this planet, at this time, with the continents and stars in their current configuration, you do not need to go this far out to make decisions about the right tools for your company's training program. But in terms of an eye-opening read about our assumptions about capturing and preserving expertise, it is well worth a weekend of your time.

When it comes to preserving the value that your company offers its customers today, and perhaps humanity tomorrow, it pays to be smart about objectively assessing the long-term value of your expertise.

If you think your product or process is passé, think again. Kodak went bankrupt, but some of its technology is still prized; the film and chemical company announced plans to re-release its iconic Super 8 camera, the grandfather of today's video. Vinyl audio records have made a comeback in the age of audio streaming. And who knows what other quaint technology might capture the fancy of a generation removed once or twice from ours? Or what technology we now consider quaint might become an important alternative in a future where some of our most advanced technology is no longer operational for a time.

If you have a cool proprietary technology that was widely used and once considered the industry standard, it might be wise to talk to some of the experts who are still around who were in on the research, development, manufacture, sales, marketing, and supply chain sourcing for that cool thing so someday, somebody can retrace your steps.

Just in case.

Learning Librarian as Content Curator

Before we completely leave the topic of preserving arcane but valuable knowledge, consider the new kinds of roles for training and development in an age of rapid learning and knowledge acquisition at the speed of light. Like a museum curator, your learning librarian's role can expand to become one whose job goes beyond cataloguing your training assets.

When your training assets have relevance beyond the curriculum in your corporate course catalogue, you need someone with a knowledge of the fields in which you are working to be able to intelligently assemble content and lead learners to the information they seek. Your content curator needs to be someone intimately familiar with content who can assemble it in ways that are accessible no matter how someone requests it, where they request it from, or in what format they need it.

Even though your content curator works in the 21st century, the concept of the role harkens back to the educated museum curator who could make informed judgments about selection, placement, relative importance, and so on of prized artifacts. When you envision this role from the perspective of working with experts, a great content curator is more likely to come from the ranks of your experts than from your training department. However, a content curator will bridge that divide between your employees and your training department, ensuring that the right information makes it into the right placement in your company's taxonomy of information assets.

8

ASSESSING FUTURE LEARNING NEEDS IN AN AGE OF INDUSTRIAL DISLOCATION

As mentioned in the previous chapter, not all knowledge needs to be preserved for business continuity. Although this book is dedicated to preserving the expertise in your organization for its competitive advantage value, as we have stated, it is still important to capture and stratify your internal knowledge using filters such as non-essential, essential, and critical knowledge. Based on the stratification exercises, you will be able to decide what you need to capture to continue your enterprise as it exists today, making the products you make today or the ones you expect your business will be making tomorrow based on what you currently know about the way your business or industry is changing.

Preserving what you think you will need in the future is a very important topic in light of the pace of change. This chapter is a small taste of an entire business genre built around the science of innovation. For this purpose, here are several lists of things to think about as you decide what to preserve in light of the pace of technological advances.

Ask yourself what might fall off your list of critical knowledge that you currently believe must be captured today. I wrote a little eBook called *30 Days to the New Economy** that explores what your business might look like as you consider the future from your vantage point today.

Peer around Corners into the Future

When you consider the kind of expertise you need to capture for your enterprise to thrive in the future, part of your job is to polish

---

* Available as a Kindle eBook at https://www.amazon.com/30-Days-New-Economy-entrepreneur-ebook/dp/B00ZSHOTBG/ref=sr_1_1?s=books&ie=UTF8&qid=147 7938203&sr=1-1&keywords=30+Days+to+the+New+Economy.

your crystal ball and determine what will be needed in a time in which you are not yet living. This requires a Zen mind trick of being able to see around corners. If you are in a position in your organization where you are in any leadership role, you need to be considering all your actions against the backdrop of what tomorrow may bring. The long view gets short shrift in management circles these days, but actually it is the long view that informs your short-term planning to avoid waste, missteps, and outright poor decisions that can lead you off a cliff.

Long-term strategic planning requires critical thinking as a type of expertise all its own, one that you can teach and grow quickly within your organization. One of the greatest values that a true critical thinker can bring to the organization is the ability to look without fear or favor at all parts of your business. That requires turning a bright light on a series of questions that will illuminate where you are and where your business is headed.

Your big picture thinking about your business and industry needs to include your knowledge management plan, or more specifically, what expertise you need to bottle and preserve to keep your organization running.

When it comes to your knowledge management plan, you need to engage unblinking honesty about the state of your business and your industry. Because, quite frankly, not everything that got you here will get you there.

The future is moving faster than the average long-term plan, which is why long-term planning has fallen out of favor to agile product development and rapid prototyping. Plans be d*****d. Your competitors have something coming off the proverbial drawing boards that can send your product off in another direction or off the market completely.

However, it bears repeating that long-term strategic planning goes hand in hand with your knowledge management planning efforts. One is not complete without the other. After you have identified where your enterprise is most likely headed, you will know what you need to preserve. You will also know what you need to acquire.

After you have completed long-term strategic planning, you may look back on a proud history of success, and you may conclude that the future will look like the past. "We have always done it that way" is an answer that might work in your business or industry as shown in this Storytime about a very unique and specialized product. But it is more likely that you do not have a heritage business and will need to make some judgments about what information is worth preserving as you anticipate change.

STORYTIME

C. F. Martin and Co. is located in Nazareth, Pennsylvania near my home. The name, Martin, is synonymous with premium acoustic guitars. The company builds its guitars today the same way it made them when the founder built the first models in 1833. If you are ever visiting the area, the factory tour is well worth your time. You can watch craftsmen and craftswomen plying their skill. The tour provides an excellent demonstration showing how a craft survives through the centuries. A Martin guitar has inestimable value for players and collectors because the instrument ages in a way that it becomes more valuable and sounds better with each passing year. Today, the guitars are built in a new replica of the original factory building, and the company is led by modern management and forward-thinking owners whose goal is to make future products with the same care and in the same way that they have always been built.

The challenge for those who have built a strong business on one set of assumptions is to realize that those assumptions may not be valid tomorrow – or even still be valid today.

If you need proof that your assumptions are probably outdated, you only need be 30 years old. The technology you experienced as a child is vastly different than the technology that permeates your everyday life today. You learned your early computer skills at a Compaq™ computer running an Intel 486 chip. *What????* Today, you are chasing Pokémon™ around O'Hare Airport on your smartphone when your flight is delayed. That pace of change is unlikely to slow anytime soon. In fact, it is hard to imagine a time when progress will slow because there is so much "there" left.

Recently, physicists transported a particle from one place to another. That experiment is the early fringe of teleporting matter. We are not there yet, but every discovery and invention changes the future. While it is not the focus of this book, I ask that you stop and consider for a New York minute (which is pretty darn quick for those of you unfamiliar with the expression) how teleportation might affect the transport of goods.

Restocking the International Space Station? No problem. Already 3D printing is addressing some of those issues. Yes, folks, that is where we are headed. So if you are building jet engines in Seattle today, ask yourself what you might be building tomorrow and where might you be building it. And just for fun, ask yourself if you will need any humans to perform those tasks. The answers to those questions are not 50 years in the future. The answers lie in work being done today.

What Business Are You Really In?

Business consultants who assist companies in business planning usually include an exercise that asks executives and owners to reach deep down into their mission and vision statements to unearth the business they are really in. One of the most often cited examples is Eastman Kodak, which started life as a chemical company that became a film and camera company. Kodak was synonymous with photography in the mid-20th century. Then digital photography happened and Kodak went bankrupt. Why did Kodak go bankrupt? The business school answer is that the company did not know what business they were in.

If Kodak concluded it was a chemical and film company, indeed digital photography spelled its death. However, if Kodak had instead concluded it was in the business of preserving images and memories, it would have thrived in the digital world. In fact, a Kodak engineer introduced one of the first digital cameras to the Kodak executive team in the late 1970s, and the team perceived it as a threat to its business and they deep-sixed it. They were half right.

The moral of the story is that Kodak executives did not recognize the business they were in. However, copier companies picked up the digitization of images and thrived making digital cameras. Likewise, cell phone companies picked up the importance of preserving memories and incorporated the technology into mobile phones. Today, your phone is your camera and a copier company makes freestanding cameras all because of the way they interpreted their mission and the business they were in.

A coda to the Kodak story is that there is a re-emergence of an interest in film photography which is why Kodak is resurrecting some of its iconic products like the Super 8 camera for a niche hobbyist market. However, the slight resurgence in no way compensates Kodak for its fall from the heights of market domination to a niche boutique business.

Business survival exists in unearthing your mission as you develop your strategic plan.

Kodak as the Poster Child for #InnovationFail

In business management and tech circles, it is often said that Kodak lost its edge in photography due to its failure to recognize two things:

1. The pace and direction of technological change, in this case the potential for digital photography and the speed at which the new technology was advancing, and
2. The business it was really in, which was capturing memories, not producing cameras, film, and chemicals.

When you are looking around your organization, do not assume that you can read the tea leaves regarding the pace of change, the direction the change will take, or the ongoing need for your goods and services. Look at changes in your market. Think about what knowledge under your roof needs to be preserved. Think big and think outside the proverbial box. My response to "Think outside the box" is "Box? What box?" If you see what you think are the edges of reality, you are only beginning to see where the future is already unfolding.

Here is an example of "no box" thinking. Let us say you are in the transportation business and you own a fleet of seafaring frigates. You might be curious about how the movement of goods around the globe could be impacted when – not if – matter can be transported from one place to another without a vehicle. Might you invest in R&D in a physics lab? Might you consider how the ability to 3D print products onsite could impact the movement of goods and services? Does the future of 3D printers that print food belong to a copier company, a food manufacturer, a chemical company, a wholesale grocery distribution company, or some other kind of business?

What is the future of the products in your industry?

What business are you in?

The answer to those questions leads to an exploration of the kinds of internal expertise you might want to capture today while you fine tune the vision of your mission. As you make judgment calls about whether to allocate finite resources to capture knowledge, skills, and attitudes, remember that Kodak engineer who developed one of the first digital cameras as you look at the kind of knowledge you want to retain.

This exercise will also lead you to thinking about the kinds of expertise you do not have under your roof right now, and whether you might want to acquire it.

For now, capture your existing information assets in light of your strategic plan and leave open the possibility that your not too distant future may look nothing like your not too distant past.

A Word about Historical Preservation

The moral of the coda of the Kodak story for this audience is that it is important to catalogue and preserve how you do everything that is unique to your company, even if it is just for historical value. Someday, someone, somewhere might want to resurrect your technology or reconstruct your products, even something as obscure as Super8 film. Make sure that what you do today can be recreated tomorrow; think like a curator of your own company's museum.

However, in the hierarchy of knowledge needs, make sure you are first capturing the knowledge and expertise you need to continue your enterprise work today. The goal of this book is to make sure you are capturing what you need for your business to thrive this year, next year, and in the coming decade.

When you are deciding what knowledge to capture and preserve, you have to make decisions based on the limited resources you can dedicate to the task. Considering that you will have some restrictions on resource allocation for knowledge capture, be sure to dedicate your first efforts to preserving the knowledge that is critical to support current business. Immediately following, engage your strategic plan to project the knowledge you need to acquire or capture to assure your continued business success. Only after you have secured your marketplace advantage can or should you turn your attention to preserving knowledge for historical purposes and the ability to reconstruct your products, services, and other assets after they have outlived their usefulness as a revenue generating asset (Figure 8.1).

After you have met your Level 1 and Level 2 immediate, critical needs for business continuity, then you can revisit aging or outdated technology and preserve it in a bit more leisurely fashion as historical artifact. I am not diminishing the importance of historical preservation by relegating it to third tier importance. What you do, even if you think it is common and unexceptional, could become uncommon and exceptional 100 years from now. But in light of where to spend finite, valuable corporate resources in the immediate present, be sure to secure your position in the marketplace so you have a history to revisit later.

For example, car and airplane rebuilders and restorers today rely on accurate schematics to recreate vintage models. In restoration and rebuilding, detail is important. Restorers are often working from blueprints or other static schematics with information written in a time when certain knowledge, skills, and tools were assumed, and other knowledge, skills, and tools were still unknown. Because yesterday's common knowledge is not common today, rebuilders and restorers are sometimes guessing how a certain thing was done and what the original designer intended by archaic directions and markings on the

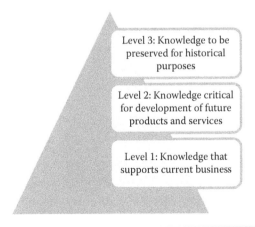

Figure 8.1 Knowledge capture activities by immediate relevance

blueprints. Do you think that the designers and builders of the Model T Ford could have imagined the pace of change and the form that automobile design and technology would take in just a few decades? I doubt it. From that limited perspective in the 1920s, they would not have codified in a stepwise fashion what they assumed to be common, unchangeable knowledge. You know better now.

I worked on a project celebrating the donation of the largest collection of antique cookbooks in the world by Esther Areste to the University of Pennsylvania Van Pelt Library. Mrs. Areste and her husband traveled the world collecting ancient cookbooks and the collection boasts the oldest known cookbooks in existence. To honor the Arestes' donation, the library's development office held a dinner honoring the couple. For the dinner, university chefs recreated recipes from some of the oldest cookbooks in the collection dating back to the 1500s and earlier. Measurements were imprecise by today's standards. The chefs worked from descriptions they were not able to accurately discern with certainty, creating recipes requiring tools no longer commonly available, and including foods no longer available or easily sourced. The chefs performed an extraordinary feat by closely recreating archaic recipes, making substitutions and adaptations so the foods were pleasant to modern palates.

Consider the hurdles that might be incurred by people recreating your knowledge at some other time, in another context, without your frames of technological, social, or historical reference. No, it is not an easy task, but it is one that is worthwhile if you have determined that the information you possess has timeless value.

Rebuilders, restorers, reenactors, and museum curators will all testify: When preserving anything for historical accuracy, be as specific as possible and make no assumptions. You will still fall short of the mark when your great-great-great-great grandchildren attempt to recreate your products for the family museum, but they will get a lot closer as a result of your efforts to preserve KSAs of inestimable value today.

When you are preserving for history, assume nothing. Capture it all. And think about what medium might still be accessible 100 years from now. If you recorded instructions for how to rebuild the carburetor on your 1968 Pontiac Firebird on an 8-track tape, you understand the unanticipated limitations of your frames of reference and methods of information capture. Gathering your critical internal expertise for transfer requires putting it through this last filter of historical importance.

Later, after you have put your competitive advantages through the many filters in this book and captured all your critical internal knowledge for business continuity and historical value, throw a retirement party for the subject matter expert who intimately understands your products and business today. After you have captured his or her expertise, you can relax and enjoy the festivities as he toddles off to a well-earned retirement in Phoenix to play golf in January.

PART III

THE NATURE OF EXPERTISE AND THE ART OF MANAGING EXPERTS

9

THE NATURE OF EXPERTISE

The respect you give others is a dramatic reflection of the respect you give yourself.

Robin Sharma, *writer and leadership speaker,*
author of The Monk Who Sold His Ferrari

While writing this book, my eye was drawn to all things that included the words "subject matter expert" and "knowledge management." I saw several titles of workshops on how to work with SMEs that bothered me. Some content reduced experts to a necessary evil who interfere with the work of trainers, instructional designers, and content developers. As a lover of experts, I have to start this section on how to work with experts by emphasizing the fact that we are lucky to have them in our midst and can be honored to work with them. After all, we would still be reading by candlelight and riding horses to visit the next village if it were not for experts.

Because of the often poisonous attitude that some practitioners in the training field harbor toward experts, I feel the need to start this section by stepping forward to speak up in defense of experts. I will not call out the sponsors of workshops or authors of books, but I will call out the pattern of disrespect because it offends me to see experts insulted. In fact, let me suggest that if people who work with experts do not respect the people they work with or enjoy their jobs, they should find other work or change their attitudes.

Here are real examples:

- One workshop offered help on how to work with "brilliant jerks." Seriously? If you think someone is a jerk, why would you want to work with him or her? Even more poignantly, why in the world do you think *he* or *she* would want to work with *you?* When you resort to name calling, it demeans not only the other person but it demeans yourself.

- Another workshop insinuated it will help you deal with experts in a way that suggested deer hunting or working in a morgue. This particular company said it can help you "snag, tag, and bag" your expert. The image is really quite macabre when you think about it.
- A third consultant suggested that experts are sort of goofy and need to be managed in a way that is downright manipulative.

A Real Methodology for Working with SMEs that Respects Everyone

Yes, good people skills are essential to working with experts. In fact, good "soft skills" – as they are called in the training industry – help in all relationships. Some trainers specialize in working with experts from a soft skills perspective and can help you "lead" experts in a relationship of mutual respect. In this next section, we will discuss strategies and tactics from this positive approach.

Some trainers, instructional designers, and content developers emphasize honing your soft skills when working with experts, but let me suggest an approach here that marries relationship prowess with process, templates, and methodology. This section recognizes the need to integrate both approaches and the value of having a combination of process and people skills in any project.

Your training project will benefit from the sensitive way you work with, talk to, and talk about the experts you have the honor of knowing and learning from. A respectful attitude ultimately spells the success or failure of your knowledge capture efforts. More importantly, your respectful attitude toward your experts is an extension of the attitude that leads to success or failure in life.

So if you think you are working with a "brilliant jerk," guess who the real "jerk" might be?

#Lectureoff

Now, let's discuss how to best work with experts for capturing, preserving, and transferring their knowledge with respect and dignity.

The Trouble with SMEs

The trouble with SMEs starts when experts look up from the petri dish or financial spreadsheet and try to tell you what they are doing.

While they are rattling on about *HARP* and *bundling* and *translational research*, you are looking at them and thinking, "Huh?" They have reached a level of expertise in which they are Unconscious Competents – that is, they are so well-informed on their subjects they do not even realize how much they know. It is likely that the expert you are working with has forgotten more than you will ever know about the content of the program you are writing.

This is a gift and a curse. Here is why.

The Four Stages of Learning Model and Your SME

In case you are not familiar with the levels of competence,[*] here are the types of competence you may encounter:

1. Unconscious Incompetent – does not know what she does not know
2. Conscious Incompetent – knows what she does not know
3. Conscious Competent – knows what she knows
4. Unconscious Competent – does not know what she knows

According to the four stages of learning model in Figure 9.1, the Unconscious Competent is the highest level of mastery on an ascending trajectory of knowledge. For that reason, these very smart people are usually assigned the job of acting as your SME for knowledge capture. However, when you look at these four stages of learning on a chart that tracks both *knowledge* and *awareness* in Figure 9.2, you can see where your master SME might fall short of your ideal SME for the purposes of gathering information in a systematic way.

The ideal SME is one that has a high level of knowledge about the subject you are capturing and a high level of awareness about what she knows. Her awareness of her knowledge makes it easier to discuss what she knows in a logical way to a novice.

---

[*] The four levels of competence are known in training literature as The Four Stages of Learning. Noel Burch of Gordon Training International is credited with developing this model in the 1970s. Others, such as Abraham Maslow, have also been credited with developing it.

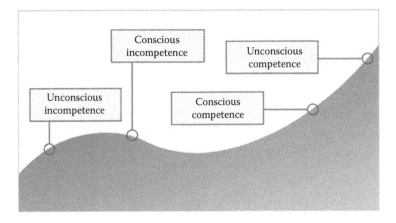

Figure 9.1   The four stages of learning

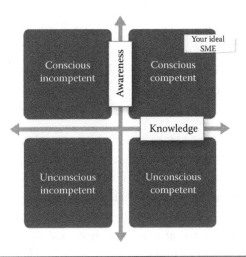

Figure 9.2   Identifying your ideal SME

Managing Experts

Experts can be your best friends for knowledge capture. But not everybody sees it that way, especially innovators. In this age of the rise of innovation and entrepreneurship as the destiny of every man, some people disrespect and disregard retiring experts because they know so much of what is known to be true today.

The age of innovation and entrepreneurship is all about developing and discovering the new, the cutting edge, the never before seen or done.

In fact, one of my living heroes, Peter H. Diamandis, coauthor of two groundbreaking books in innovation – *Bold* and

Abundance – recommended, in a May 14, 2017 Tech Blog, that when companies want to do something new and disruptive, they need to avoid their experts. His reasoning is logical. Experts know a lot about the status quo; after all, they have likely created it.

> An expert is someone who can tell you exactly how something can't be done.
>
> **Peter's Laws #21**

Your current experts will be spring-loaded to protect the status quo they have invested their careers in developing. Experts often see things from the way they are, not the way they could be. Also, they have a vested interest in the way things are because if the status quo changes; their knowledge could get relegated to the scrap heap of history.

This logic dictates that you do not want experts on your team creating innovative, disruptive products. When a company wants to move beyond the now, it needs to bring in new minds to the problem that can see it in a fresh way.

Diamandis is right. He is my hero. Of course, I think he is right. After all, he is among an elite group that gave us the XPrize, Singularity University, and he is squarely in front of the human potential movement.

He even quotes Henry Ford, that icon of innovation, here:

> I will close this blog with a quote from Henry Ford…I LOVE this quote. Enjoy.
>
> None of our men are "experts." We have most unfortunately found it necessary to get rid of a man as soon as he thinks himself an expert because no one ever considers himself an expert if he really knows his job. A man who knows a job sees so much more to be done than he has done, that he is always pressing forward and never gives up an instant of thought to how good and how efficient he is. Thinking always ahead, thinking always of trying to do more, brings a state of mind in which nothing is impossible. The moment one gets into the "expert" state of mind, a great number of things become impossible.
>
> Keep innovating and let's create a world of Abundance.

So says Peter quoting Henry. But fire your experts? That seems a bit rash. Maybe you want to hold off on that. Let us discuss.

Yes, you probably do not want your seasoned veterans leading the team that is tasked with coming up with the next great thing – your "Moonshot" – to borrow Diamandis' language.

To further quote Diamandis in an email to his followers, he wrote of another innovation icon on September 3, 2017:

> My definition of an entrepreneurial or corporate Moonshot comes from my friend Astro Teller, who is the current head of X (formerly Google X).
>
> He defines it as going 10X bigger, while the rest of the world is trying to grow 10%.
>
> As Astro described it, most executive teams aim for 10% growth... they'll work harder, buy new equipment, work nights or weekends, and try to eke out 10% growth.
>
> A Moonshot (10x improvement), in contrast, can't be achieved by working harder alone.
>
> You have to start with a clean sheet of paper and be willing to try seemingly crazy ideas.
>
> You have to keep writing down crazy ideas until you find one that doesn't actually seem so crazy.
>
> Don't forget that "the day before something is truly a breakthrough, it's a crazy idea."

Thus spoke Diamandis.

While your next Moonshot may not be led by your seasoned experts, let me suggest that existing experts in the field know a lot about what has worked and what did not. Or... at least your experts know what has not worked in the past given the limitations of the knowledge and resources available at the time certain ideas were tested.

Innovation requires both a strong knowledge of what was and what is in order to provide a solid foundation to comprehend what could be.

This is why.

Sometimes the reason something was done, or was not done, is not immediately obvious. You can save hours, days, weeks, years, and millions of dollars when you find out why, for example, you need to process something by etching or printing. Why water works in the process or did not at the time. Why certain batteries failed at a point in the process. Why humans just would not do it that way. What happens when you incentive using gift cards. And so on. And so on.

Perhaps another way to see the issue of Henry Ford's admonition to "Fire Your Experts!" is to suggest that you enlist them as historical resources. Go to them. Ask them questions. You may hear things like, "Oh, we tried that and we were surprised that they bought less of this and more of that due to X," or "It took twice as long because we didn't foresee Y," or "Customers were driven to a competitor because of Z."

Your current fresh minds working on solutions will know if the limitations or parameters when it was last tried have changed enough over the last 5, 20, 50, or 70 years that problems encountered then may no longer exist today.

Experts house history between their ears.

Those who don't know history are destined to repeat it.

British statesman and philosopher Edmund Burke (1729–1797)

Therefore, I might slightly modify Ford's and Diamandis' suggestions to say that if you want to do something new and disruptive, have your fresh talent go at it full bore with a clean slate. And have your experts on call to backstop them and answer questions.

If your fresh talent and your seasoned experts can put their egos on the shelf and are not worried about protecting their reputations as brilliant young engineers or defending the status quo as they created it years ago, you may find that the one-two combo platter of shiny new genius and seasoned expert are an unbeatable team.

Figure 9.3 shows the blending of seasoned experts with your brilliant new talent to achieve expedited innovation in your organization.

Expedited, innovative product

Figure 9.3 Masterful mix: Blending seasoned experts and brilliant new talent

10

KNOWLEDGE CAPTURE USING EXPERTS WITHIN THE PROVEN ADDIE FRAMEWORK

A process set up anywhere, reverberates everywhere.

US psychologist and philosopher
William James [1842–1910]

After you have identified the critical information you need to capture for business continuity and the people who know it, it is time to put a process in place to work with your experts for knowledge capture.

While these processes work with experts for any purpose of cataloguing their expertise, this section discusses capturing expert knowledge specifically for training since knowledge transfer is a large part of the purpose behind corporate knowledge capture.

As part of the information collection process, training departments usually develop templates for review cycles and signoffs with subject matter experts. Some recommendations for processes and checklists are included later in this section.

A training program has two parts:

1. Instructional design is how to *structure and relate* knowledge, skills, and attitudes (KSAs) in a systematic way.
2. *Working with SMEs* is about how to *collect* information from the *right* people, *select* what is relevant, and *organize it* in a systematic way.

Instructional designers have their favorite models for designing training and they usually apply some variation of the ADDIE (Analysis, Design, Development, Implementation, and Evaluation) model. The *Working with SMEs* methodology for collecting information is built on ADDIE and includes the expert's involvement in all aspects of it.

Initially, the intense information gathering phase begins at Analysis in which you collect most information from subject matter experts. Content gathering carries through the ADDIE process as you organize content and refine your program through Development to Evaluation, including review cycles and sign-off milestones.

Specifically, in the Analysis phase, you determine the breadth and scope of the project you are undertaking. You list resources, including the people who will serve as your subject matter experts. During this preliminary phase, the information you gather influences the project scope based on what you are learning. At this point, subject matter experts provide you with data, notes, and information that you may be supplementing with focus groups, surveys, and other data collection tools.

By the time you reach the Design phase, project specifications are driven by your audience, learning objectives and the activities that are best suited to achieve your overall performance goals.[*] During this phase, clients[†] approve graphics, software, and any other criteria for presentation of the program. SMEs are important in the review cycle to ensure the material does not distort the intent of the subject matter.

During Development, you rely heavily on experts to ensure as you build out the Design that you adhere to the plan and add only relevant material in an accurate and compelling way. After Development, both the SMEs and the project stakeholders should sign off on all phases of the project before implementation.

During Implementation, experts can often serve as program facilitators and resources when learners and program developers have content questions that inevitably arise during presentation of the material.

Ideally, the formal Evaluation phase occurs at least 30–60 days after Implementation to find out if learning "stuck." Based on the

---

[*] We use the term *performance goals* for the high-level behavioral objectives of the training program; some training designers may use other terms such as *terminal objectives*.

[†] The term, client, refers to the entity that is paying for the training program. If you are a training company, the client is an external customer; if you are a training department in a large organization, the client is an internal customer or department.

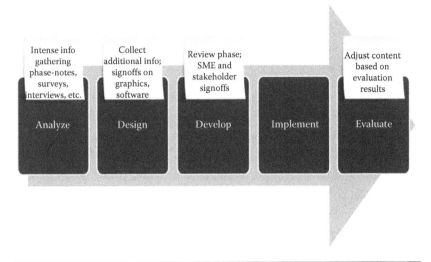

Figure 10.1 Working with SMEs in the ADDIE methodology

results of the Evaluation, the program may require content adjustments which frequently involve a second, abbreviated iteration of the ADDIE process.

While instructional designers use different methodologies, the ADDIE model provides all the elements of well thought out training even if the individual components are not specifically identified. Even if you use another abbreviated method or one with a different cycle pattern, ADDIE captures all the phases that are inherent in the other models.

The following Figure 10.1 is a snapshot of the expert's involvement at each point in the ADDIE process.

Your Assigned SME and the ADDIE Process

As the term implies, the assigned subject matter expert is dedicated to helping you build the training program or provide information for knowledge capture. An expert is helpful, in fact necessary, at all phases of building your training program. Therefore, here is a more detailed description of your expert's involvement.

If you are an internal training department in an engineering firm, the expertise you need is already your firm's core competency. It is expected that your SMEs are available when you need them. However, if your internal experts do not have the time to dedicate to holding your hand throughout each phase of training, you can consider hiring a dedicated subject matter expert to assist as a backup and as a second opinion when you need one.

The SME's role in the ADDIE process:

1. Analyze phase: The expert is present to ask questions and help direct the conversations about the training topic.
2. Design phase: The expert helps organize the content and clarify the objectives.
3. During data collection, the expert provides information and checks the client's materials for accuracy, clarity, and gaps.
4. Development phase: The expert does the first "content dump" by putting the material in your framework.
5. Development phase: The expert validates your activities and assessment tests.
6. Implementation phase: Especially in the case of instructor led training, the expert may also serve as a facilitator for the program due to her expertise and is available to answer questions when the content reaches the learner.
7. Evaluation phase: The expert can work with your instructional design experts to assess the program's effectiveness and participate in adjustments to the course material.

When to Use a Dedicated SME: Handholding

Considering the extensive value of your expert over the life of your training project, you may need or want to hire an expert whose sole responsibility is to work with you to build your training program.

If you are a training and organizational development company working as an external consultant to build a training program, you may want to hire a Dedicated SME to act as an on call consultant to provide you with the kind of expertise you need to deliver a top quality training program. A Dedicated SME does not replace any internal or client experts who have intimate knowledge of the business you have identified in the exercises in Part I to find your SMEs. However, an expert who works only on training is available to fill in and reinforce the information you need to fully and accurately develop course work.

Using a Dedicated SME does not alter any of the process steps for *Working with SMEs,* but it gives the instructional designer confidence and a dependable resource when wading in unfamiliar or intimidating topic areas by having a subject matter expert assigned solely to assist her in writing her training program.

Here are a few situations in which you may want to consider using a Dedicated SME:

- When the training designers are not confident that they can understand a complex or intimidating topic using the regular steps for *Working with SMEs*
- When your client SMEs may not be available for the amount of time you need to fully understand your topic due to the demands of their regular assignments
- When your client SMEs may not have time for thorough reviews of your material
- When your client SMEs are in disagreement and differences in materials need to be negotiated.

Things to consider when hiring a Dedicated SME:

- You are sure that the subject matter is incomprehensible to you without one.
- The project price supports it and the client is willing to pay for it (this is true for both consulting firms and internal training department budgets).
- The Dedicated SME works well with the client's SMEs.
- The SME supports the firm's training mission and fits into the culture.
- You are certain that there are not enough SMEs with enough time in the organization you are working with to help you gather and review the content.

A Dedicated SME can be a valuable asset in helping you create a strong product when those conditions exist. As an added bonus, if you are an external training consultant, after you have hired a SME in a specific topic area, you have now strengthened your hand in that field and can attract other clients with similar needs. It is a move you may consider when you are building competency as a single topic training design house.

The cost and dedication to this effort is substantial, but if you are working with a client who is willing to pay for you to acquire this competency, you can yield the benefits without incurring the cost.

Considerations for a *Working with SMEs* Methodology

The core of the model for *Working with SMEs* establishes what good information gathering looks like. A best practices model should contain these four elements that are common to all content gathering efforts for any knowledge capture project.

A Working with SMEs methodology:

1. Provides instructional designers and content developers a framework for collecting and reviewing content with your subject matter expert
2. Describes the qualities of a good SME and how to work with them
3. Works within the existing system (for example, if you are an instructional designer, it would work with ADDIE,) and takes into account the already existing body of knowledge and commonly accepted best practices
4. Includes a framework for managing the content collection and review cycles

Taking those requirements into consideration, this methodology is structured around meeting these goals.

Let us begin our journey in developing a methodology for *Working with SMEs* by first defining The Perfect SME so we have a springboard for identifying deficits and the need for adjustments in the process.

The Perfect SME has three essential qualities. He or she is:

- The most knowledgeable and articulate person about that topic in the organization
- One who has, or will be given, the time to work with you
- Willing (and possibly looking forward) to being part of the training design process

If your SME is missing any of these three ingredients, you will encounter resistance to efficiently and accurately gathering the information you need. If you have a less than perfect SME and you do not have access to an alternate expert, we offer tips and tools throughout this section to help you negotiate those issues effectively.

First, whether you have been dealt the Perfect SME or not, you will need to establish deadlines and clear lines of communication for fact checking and sign offs at the very beginning of your relationship. It is unlikely the SME will be tracking those things, and you may not have other supports in place to do it for you. Your project scope or project charter should include details about deadlines and lines of responsibility that can help define the relationship upfront.

As the instructional designer on the project, you will find yourself managing up, managing laterally, and possibly managing outside your department to make things happen. Setting expectations and deadlines before you begin will make the process smoother and less harrowing for you and those working with you.

Which brings us back to the trouble with SMEs...yes, even the perfect ones who meet all three of the essential qualities.

The Content Developer's Job When Working with Experts

When you are working with subject matter experts whether to build a training program, write marketing and sales materials, or write their books for them, your job is to help them think in a linear way so your product is clear and transfers their information correctly.

Your job is threefold:

1. Establish and agree upon the goals for the project.
2. Determine the parameters of the information to be included.
3. Create a timetable and process for achieving completion.

When those three goals are firmly in front of the content developer and the expert, you should be able to capture everything you need in a way that makes it easy to understand and transfer later.

It is the content developer's job to ask a lot of questions. He may be trying to get context and may ask a lot of questions to tie the learning to other things. In adult learning for example, it is good practice to give context to learners by relating new knowledge to things they already know. That means that an instructional designer may look for touchpoints in the expert content. However, whenever a content developer is trying to draw parallels or make connections that wander too far afield to be relevant, the expert should speak up and tell him so.

Conversely, and probably more commonly, the content developer or instructional designer may not be asking enough questions. He may not know to ask certain questions to help him gain context and background. If an expert is talking and the content developer has a quizzical look, it is time for the expert to stop and ask if he needs clarification. The content developer may be waiting for the punchline or, possibly, may have lost the thread completely and does not know what to ask to find his way back.

A good content developer will be organized. He will collect and document information so he does not have to go back to the SME multiple times. It is up to the expert to review the material to make sure it is in context, accurate, and really needs to be included. The review process ensures the information included is well understood and presented appropriately at each step of the information collection process.

The content developer is responsible for assembling questions, proposing an interview and review schedule, and asking the expert to fill in gaps in knowledge. The process may not always happen flawlessly, but it can happen with relative ease when both the content creator and the expert have the same vision at the outset.

Help the expert by providing a list of activities that will help him or her give the content developer some foundational knowledge. Experts want their knowledge transferred accurately and the process to be as painless as possible.

This section later includes two tear sheet ideas to share with your experts to help them participate in information gathering. One tear sheet helps your expert comply with your information gathering process by outlining what to expect. The second tear sheet helps your expert provide information in a linear way that is most useful to the content developer who is unfamiliar with the subject matter.* The lists

---

* As an aside and therefore footnote, scientists are learning how to communicate within their own communities and with the public about their work. For example, a conference sponsored by the National Academy of Sciences, The Science of Communication III, offers two days of workshops and lectures on how to communicate complex information. The NAS also publishes a series of books on how to communicate scientific information.

are generic. You can use and adapt these sheets to your organization, your process, and your language.

While this section provides some aids and advice for the expert, the majority of the process steps focus on the content developer's role. In the next chapters, you will find detailed lists, charts, templates, and checklists that content developers and instructional designers can use to put structure around the knowledge capture process.

11

MANAGING THE 10
TYPES OF EXPERTS

Experts are as varied as humanity itself, which means the actual expression of their genius is almost infinite. In my experience, 10 broad categories of types of experts have emerged and they include most of the human variations. This chapter offers recommendations for working with experts that fall into one of these 10 categories.

Like any plan or process, you will want to adjust these recommendations for your circumstance. For some people, these plans are too formal and structured and using only the essence of the ideas here will be enough to accomplish your goals. For others, the plans may not be detailed enough. In that case, you can build on the concepts to create a plan that meets your more complex objectives. For most however, the plans and checklists in here should be just about right for your project.

Because this chapter is intended for application as opposed to theoretical discussion, it includes perhaps more detail than you might need in your particular situation. It also includes places to take notes and add your own details pertinent to your project if you are applying these recommendations to your work.

The concepts are intended to simplify a methodology for working with experts. In your reality, you are dealing with more complex issues, humans of varying temperaments with different agendas, and companies struggling with a host of issues that often have little time or patience for training and development while they juggle many urgent and competing operational priorities. In your reality, you do not live in a simple world. But in your role in the real world, if you can find even a few processes and templates to help you approach a problem regarding knowledge transfer in a methodical way, then this chapter will have met its goal.

Let us start by expanding the definition of The Perfect SME so we have best practices against which to gauge the methods suggested herein.

Encountering the Perfect SME

Like all things perfect, The Perfect Subject Matter Expert exists only as an ideal. However, most of the experts I have met are genuinely brilliant, helpful, and generous human beings, and they are wonders to behold.

When you encounter The Perfect SMEs, you will find they:

- Are really, really smart and know more about their subjects than anybody else in your universe
- Are willing, able, and looking forward to serving as experts for your project
- Can tell you what they know in a logical way
- Understand why it is important for other people to know what they know
- Are on time for appointments
- Appreciate that they are part of a team and know that other people's schedules often depend on theirs
- Meet review cycles
- Are approachable and often fun to work with
- Love to teach their subjects and make great presenters or facilitators
- Stay current in their areas of expertise
- Know when to refer you to someone else

And now for those times when life interferes with perfection...

In the real world, people have competing obligations, bad days, lives outside work, pressure from others to skew what they know to meet slanted agendas, and on and on and on.

For all people who work with experts who live in the real world, the following pages are intended to help navigate those times when you are called to ask experts to cooperate in knowledge transfer and life interferes.

The Speedy SME's Defining Characteristics

Pitfall: The Speedy SME becomes impatient with you controlling the pace of the session. Most likely, this expert has many competing demands on his time. Your request for his time to recount what he knows may be a laborious and painful process for them. Promising new projects call this expert, important meetings await him, and your project may be mundane to him as he retreads old ground. Your expert is impatient because he is anticipating the next, more appealing and exciting interaction.

You can face these facts and work with this SME to meet both of your objectives.

Share these tips with The Speedy SME

- You know volumes more than anyone else in the organization about your subject, so have patience with those who need to learn from you.
- Be slow and thorough; use steps whenever you can to explain what you know. If you tend not to be a methodical person, allow the person organizing your expertise to lead the process for you.
- If you have a firm stop, tell your interviewer and adjust the session to make the most of your time.

Tips for Content Developers Working with The Speedy SME

- Explain that less skilled personnel will complete the training program that you are developing. Tell your expert that you need to capture all of the details to make that possible.
- Reassure the SME that documentation will take less time if you move slowly and steadily so you can capture all the information the first time.
- Use mild humor or a gentle manner to help diffuse frustration.

To gain clarity for how to handle this situation, make a list of the particular challenges that you face with The Speedy SME. Address each one with tactics to overcome them using these principles with an issue-response list like the sample below.

Challenges	Tactics

The Creative, Scattered SME's Defining Characteristics

Pitfall: The good news is that you have a fascinating, creative person to work with who has done some very original work. The mind that creates is a right brain thinker, the side of the brain that is not logical. A creative person sees patterns, but they are not as obvious to the observer or to someone who wants to capture the genius behind the creation. The Creative, Scattered SME is often scattered, does not think sequentially, and sees the process as so complex and variable that it cannot possibly be captured in steps.

Your job is to unpack as much of the process as possible in a way that preserves their creativity without imposing too much structure on the person.

Share these tips with The Creative, Scattered SME:

- Your type of genius possibly requires that you are a right brain thinker using creative associations in your field. Be reassured that some left brain thinkers are available to dissect your subject in a way that others can understand it.
- While others may want to understand your product or process, there is a good chance they will never have your particular type of intelligence that leads to creative development. Be patient with those who may just want to understand and appreciate what you do and capture it for posterity.
- Your contributions to your company will live on to the extent you are able to help the company preserve them.

Tips for content developers working with The Creative, Scattered SME:

- Reassure the SME that it is your job to make sense out of a complex process and you have experience doing that.
- Guide the info gathering session using a process. (See interview process recommendations in the next chapter.)
- Encourage the SME to show you the steps or explain the area of knowledge so you can get a feel for the field.
- Ask questions when you do not understand.
- Be genuinely interested. Creative people love to talk about what they do because they love what they do.

To gain clarity on solutions for dealing with this situation, make a list of the particular challenges that you face with The Creative, Scattered SME. Address each one with tactics to overcome them using the principles above.

Challenges	Tactics

The Shortcut SME's Defining Characteristics

Pitfall: This will be one of the most common attributes of any expert, and you will find this in combination with other characteristics of the other types. The Shortcut SME has worked in their area of expertise for so long that he or she uses shortcuts a novice could never follow. Not only are the shortcuts a detriment to transferring knowledge accurately, but the shortcuts developed by the expert over time also might not be the best practice for the organization or the product and process.

Your job is to slow down The Shortcut SME so each step is understood, documented, and preserved in a way that is accurate and replicable.

Share these tips with The Shortcut SME:

- Slow down please.
- Provide documentation, or create a chart/outline steps/capture screen shots/create a diagram to make your knowledge easy for others to follow.
- Trust people who are skilled at documenting the expertise of others.

Tips for content developers working with The Shortcut SME:

- Refocus the SME by explaining that you are to document only best practices for the company that can be followed by the audience who will definitely include people not as experienced as the SME.
- Request the SME demonstrate the best practice process in a slow, methodical way.
- Ask the SME to provide you with an outline, steps, or documentation of the process or procedure.
- In cases where physical steps are used (such as computer actions or mechanical expertise), if you cannot get the SME to slow down, consider making a thorough video of all angles and operations, and slow it down so you have an accurate record of the action.

To gain clarity on ways to capture information whizzing by you, make a list of the particular challenges that you face with The Shortcut

SME. Address each one with tactics to overcome them using the principles above.

Challenges	Tactics

The Defensive SME's Defining Characteristics

Pitfall: Most often, The Defensive SME feels her job is threatened. She is afraid that if she shares her expertise, she runs the risk of losing her position. This is one of the most difficult experts to handle because she is driven by fear. Your job in this case is to provide reassurance and context for the collection of information.

Share these tips with The Defensive SME:

- Be assured that the definition of an expert is one that has spent at least 10,000 hours perfecting her knowledge, and you cannot be replaced that easily!
- Your contribution as your company's expert elevates you to a priceless resource as a guide for younger and less experienced workers.
- By training others to take your place, it frees you for next level tasks and promotions, if that is your goal.

Tips for content developers working with The Defensive SME:

- Reinforce the value of the SME's expertise.
- Use a nonthreatening scenario like, "Imagine that starting next week I am going to be your personal assistant, and you want me to do this task for you."
- Appreciate your expert's unique skills, knowledge, and other attributes that make her valuable to the company.

To gain clarity on how to break down resistance, make a list of the particular challenges that you face with The Defensive SME. Address each one with tactics to overcome them using the principles above.

Challenges	Tactics

The Not-Quite-Expert SME's Defining Characteristics

Pitfall: The Not-Quite-Expert SME does not really know best practice or what you are asking him about or, at least, believes that he does not know. Working with The Not-Quite-Expert SME can be very tricky. If, in the first case, The Not-Quite-Expert SME truly is not the right expert for the job – and he knows it – you can work with him or around him to find the right person. If, however, he actually has more expertise than he realizes, you can simply proceed to uncover what you need to know and, in the process, he may come to value his own expertise while working with you.

Share these tips with The Not-Quite-Expert SME:

- If you have been identified as the expert and you feel you are not suited to the task, participate in sessions with the content developer before you decide that you are not the correct expert. While you may not think you are the expert, you may well be the person who is most knowledgeable in your area or in your company.
- If you or the people working with you decide that, indeed, you do not have the knowledge to perform as the subject matter expert, help the content developer find someone who can serve as the SME. Chances are if you have been identified, you know where experts can be found.
- If you have offered yourself as an expert or someone else has recommended you, and then you determine you are not the right person to serve as a SME, be honest and tell the people you are working with so you can serve as a resource during the search process.

Tips for content developers working with The Not-Quite-Expert SME:

- If you determine that the person is not the best person with the information that you need, discuss the situation with your supervisor. Identify an alternative expert who may know the process or topic better.
- For some new processes, best practice may not yet be well established. In this case, reassure the SME that he or she is

the most qualified person in the organization at this time to help you work through the details.

- Review the resulting information with other experienced personnel including supervisors as either an interim review or part of the final review to backstop the information you have received.

To gain clarity on how to determine whether you are working with the correct expert, make a list of the particular challenges that you face with The Not-Quite-Expert SME. Address each one with tactics to overcome them using the principles above.

Challenges	Tactics

The Overcommitted SME's Defining Characteristics

Pitfall: The Overcommitted SME consistently misses or is late for appointments or is overloaded with regular work responsibilities. He or she complains about and may resent making time for the knowledge capture session and can be generally uncooperative. Some may act unpleasantly toward you. The Overcommitted SME requires patience, organization, and tact.

Share these tips with The Overcommitted SME:

- Set aside uninterrupted time for the content developer working with you. Turn off phones and email. Request that you are not interrupted. Close the door. One uninterrupted hour is worth at least 4 hours of interrupted time.
- Provide documentation, slides, video, or audio to support your work before the session. It will avoid having to repeat the session and reduce revision cycles.
- Making time to help others understand what you do ultimately raises your value and is essential to your company's long-term success.
- If you are working with an instructional designer to develop training in your area of expertise, the time you spend now to help train others will ultimately free you for higher level tasks.
- You are providing added value to the business. If you are working with a content developer – such as a writer, marketer, or public relations person – know that the time you give them will help promote you, your project or idea, and your company.

Tips for content developers working with The Overcommitted SME:

- Do your best to empathize with the expert's situation and assure her you will not waste his time.
- Make sure the SME knows what you will be doing in the information gathering session so she can have documents ready.
- Call and/or email the day before to confirm and remind the expert of the appointment.
- If the issue persists, review the situation with your supervisor. Often the SME is trying to juggle conflicting priorities.

Perhaps your supervisor can intervene and get her freed up to be available.

- Always thank the SME for his or her time and commitment.

To gain clarity on how to expedite content gathering from a busy SME, make a list of the particular challenges that you face with The Overcommitted SME. Address each one with tactics to overcome them using the principles above.

Challenges	Tactics

The Confounding SME's Defining Characteristics

Pitfall: You may not be getting all the correct information that you need because you have a SME who is an unconscious competent – she does not know what she knows - so she cannot tell you. The Confounding SME is difficult to understand. The difficulty may be the result of her inability to communicate clearly, or – in rarer cases – it may be the result of her reluctance to be forthcoming (see The Reluctant SME.) In either case, your job is to make sure the information that you are receiving is correct and complete.

Whenever you are working with The Confounding SME, you need to trust but verify. When you are working with The Confounding SME, this becomes your mantra.

Share these tips with The Confounding SME:

- What you know may be very difficult for a layperson to understand so take care to communicate in common vocabulary as much as possible. When you must use a technical term, define it.
- If your field is technical or scientific, offer foundational materials as pre-work for the content developer before meetings and interviews.
- Bring in a second person, such as a mentee or one of your students, who can act as a translator for more difficult material that you find hard to communicate to lay people.
- The clearer you can be about your expertise, the more valuable you are to your company and your colleagues in the knowledge transfer process.

Tips for content developers working with The Confounding SME:

- If you do not understand it, nobody will understand your interpretation of it. So work to make sure you are clear about the content.
- Ask for any materials related to the area of expertise such as slide presentations, audios, videos, articles, books, or diagrams before meeting.
- Ask the expert to create a diagram or write down steps to their knowledge.
- Verify incomprehensible content with other experts in the same or related fields.

- Use your own common sense if something seems too difficult to understand. You will be sharing this knowledge with others who may not know any more – or perhaps even less – than you do. If you cannot figure it out, they probably will not be able to figure it out either. Break out complex knowledge into digestible bites.

To gain clarity when the content is incomprehensible, make a list of the particular challenges that you face with The Confounding SME. Address each one with tactics to overcome them using the principles above.

Challenges	Tactics

The SME Interrupted's Defining Characteristics

Pitfall: The SME Interrupted is constantly being interrupted during the information gathering session, causing both you and the expert to lose track of what you are doing. This requires you to start again or, even worse, to forget what you planned to tackle.

Like The Overcommitted SME, The Interrupted SME may have a lot going on. But unlike The Overcommitted SME, these interruptions may not always be important or work related. The Interrupted SME may just thrive on social interaction, whether it is an endless Twitter stream or Facebook addiction. No matter the reason, if a SME is constantly interrupted, it makes for very inefficient, costly, and lengthy meetings, so it is good to have some strategies for accomplishing tasks quickly and with focus.

Share these tips with The SME Interrupted:

- Turn off phones, ignore social media, and close the door to concentrate on the content developer who needs your attention.
- Choose a time when you are least busy.
- Consider a different location than your regular work environment where you will not be interrupted.
- When you remain focused, you will avoid having to revisit the material later.
- Provide as much documentation and material as you can, either before the session or after the session to reduce the amount of time you need to spend in interview sessions.

Tips for working with The SME Interrupted:

- Reassure the SME that documentation will take less time if both of you are focused.
- Conduct the session away from the workstation. Caveat: If the task is documenting software, make sure the software and hardware functions the same in the alternate location.
- If you cannot move to a less busy location, ask the SME to forward his phone to voicemail and tack a "Do Not Disturb" sign on his cubicle or office door.

- Let the SME select the meeting time. Be flexible and work at a time when interruptions are less likely. This may be very early or late in the day.
- Limit the sessions to 2 or 3 hours at the very most, so it does not interfere with an entire work day and the SME can give you one-on-one quality time. A very busy, high demand executive is not likely to be able to carve out 2 or 3 uninterrupted hours, so content yourself with 1 hour and be well prepared to maximize the opportunity. See the checklist for tips on how to prepare for an interview in the appendix.

To gain clarity on how to create a focused session, make a list of the particular challenges that you face with The SME Interrupted. Address each one with tactics to overcome them using the principles above.

Challenges	Tactics

Reckless Reviewer's Defining Characteristics

Pitfall: The Reckless Reviewer does not check her own work, and does not check your work to make sure you have captured her expertise correctly. The Reckless Reviewer is available for just as long as it takes to check the box that confirms your request for feedback has been seen. When you are working with a Reckless Reviewer, you are not able to verify your content. One of the biggest dangers of The Reckless Reviewer is that if she also served as your subject matter expert, that careless attitude probably means that your original content is not reliable either. You need a trustworthy backstop, and if your Reckless Reviewer also served as your SME, you may need to start collecting new information from the beginning. To avoid having to start all over, if you realize you may be working with a Reckless Reviewer, take some proactive steps to mitigate the damage on the back end of your project.

Share these tips with The Reckless Reviewer SME:

- A careful review of the material will ensure that the person you are working with has captured everything correctly. The accuracy of the final product will reflect on you.
- Meet your review deadlines. Usually, several people have scheduled their work around your timely review, including editors and graphic designers. Late reviews can be costly not only in wasted time, but they can slip the schedules of other projects that people are obligated to complete.
- If you served as the original subject matter expert, recall what you said the first time and be sure to validate that content in the review. Unless you realize that you have missed relaying a critical bit of information during the content collection phase, do not add a lot of new content at the review phase which could skew other parts of the project.

Tips for content developers working with The Reckless Reviewer SME:

- Set the expectations of a thorough review up front during the information gathering phase during development.
- Spend time with The Reckless Reviewer SME to review the data in your information gathering session. For example, if it

is a physical task or software documentation, read each step and have the expert perform it. Watch for missed steps and explanations that do not match actions.

- Use a review method that is easy for the expert. For example, if the expert is comfortable writing in a Word® document, use that platform. However, if your expert is comfortable with more sophisticated software, show her how to use the review functions in software designed for training. Also be prepared to work in hard copy with highlighter and sticky notes, if necessary. If your Reckless Reviewer is comfortable with the review process that you use, she is more likely to attend to it promptly and with some degree of diligence.

To gain clarity on how to confirm the validity of the content you are receiving, make a list of the particular challenges that you face with The Reckless Reviewer SME. Address each one with tactics to overcome them using the principles above.

Challenges	Tactics

The Reluctant SME's Defining Characteristics

Pitfall: This is one of the most common problems you may encounter when working with subject matter experts. The reasons for their reluctance can be varied and many and will often overlap with other types of SME resistance, such as The Defensive SME and The Confounding SME. When you have a Reluctant SME, you may spend a lot of time breaking down walls to get her to work with you, and the source of the reluctance may not be obvious. Often The Reluctant SME has some job insecurity and may actually be a Defensive SME in disguise. For example, her reluctance may really be about her allegiance to a union or guild with strict rules that she may interpret as interference when you collect information about processes and company-specific knowledge. As a group, they may simply be afraid they will be replaced if they tell you what they know. If that is the case, they may try to confound you by speaking quickly, inaccurately, or incomprehensibly. The Reluctant SME most likely needs reassurance that her job is safe. However, leave open the possibility that The Reluctant SME may have other sources of reluctance, such as simple shyness, disability, or an illness she may be trying to disguise. Tread carefully, respect her, lay some groundwork for a trusting and respectful relationship and you can probably overcome any resistance.

Share these tips with The Reluctant SME:

- If you have been asked to serve as an expert for a project at work, it is an honor. Your company needs you and it reflects well on you to be asked and to serve.
- Anything that is particular to your job or proprietary to the company needs to be captured by the company for business continuity. If you win the lottery tomorrow and leave for Hawaii, your coworkers and, perhaps, your customers need to know where you have hidden the keys to the kingdom.
- Because you have been identified as an expert, you are very difficult to replace. In fact, an expert usually has 5 or more years on one particular job. It will take someone else a very long time – if ever – to know what you know or figure out how to do what you do. By participating in sharing your

knowledge, you are continuing your legacy and giving someone else a chance to appreciate what you have dedicated yourself to creating and perfecting.

Tips for the content developer working with The Reluctant SME:

- You are an expert, your knowledge is valuable, and your knowledge needs to be shared with others.
- You are indeed an expert and by definition, you are not easily replaced.
- Your coworkers, your customers, your business, and the public depend on you. You have spent a long time, and maybe even a lifetime, learning what you know, and sharing it is part of your gift to others.

To gain clarity on how to overcome resistance in your content gathering efforts, make a list of the particular challenges that you face with The Reluctant SME. Address each one with tactics to overcome them using the principles above.

Challenges	Tactics

When All Else Fails: The Dedicated SME or SME for Hire

This is a good place to expand and reinforce a discussion of the role of The Dedicated SME as an adjunct to your use of subject matter experts who are less than ideal. An encounter with any of the 10 Types of SMEs may trigger the need for a Dedicated SME.

A Dedicated SME is an expert hired by a firm to either supplement existing resources or to acquire expertise that is unavailable or in short supply for the sole purpose of content creation. A Dedicated SME, or SME for Hire, is not retained to actually perform the functions of the job in question (i.e., The Dedicated SME does not perform accounting functions, or serve as an engineer or sales account manager in your organization) but rather he or she is a subject matter expert source of information for developing training, sales, and marketing materials or to act as an expert in some administrative capacity such as an advisor to the CEO in the area of expertise.

Your Dedicated SME acts as an internal corporate training or information resource.

A Dedicated SME for Hire gives you access to expertise you may not be able to obtain internally for any of the 10 reasons listed earlier. As the term implies, The Dedicated SME is dedicated to helping you as a knowledge resource on a full-time or exclusive contractual basis.

NOTE: If you hire an expert as an adjunct to your internal resources, make sure to button up your confidentiality arrangements before you begin sharing information with him or her.

You may hire external experts for any number of reasons including when your internal experts are overloaded with work or may not have niche experience for the purpose you need to tap them. Sometimes, a company may hire expertise for a particular purpose under a limited contract as a consultant.

Your Dedicated SME may act as a contracted external training resource too. A Dedicated SME can be very helpful to freestanding independent training consulting firms whose core expertise is performance and organizational development but not the area of the training topic.

If, on the first hand, you are an internal training department in an engineering firm, the expertise you need is already your firm's core competency. It is expected that your full-time staff is available, so usually there is no need to hire someone just to work with the training department. It is in your company's best interest to utilize your internal experts. You only need to hire a Dedicated SME in the case your internal experts are overextended to help you on a supplemental basis or as a niche authority.

If, on the other hand, you are a full-time training and organizational development company working on a training program for an engineering firm, you may find it helpful to hire a full-time engineering consultant to provide you with the kind of expertise you need to deliver a top quality training program.

In both cases, the presence of a Dedicated SME does not alter any of the process steps for working with SMEs, but it gives the content developer confidence when wading into unfamiliar or intimidating topic areas by having a subject matter expert assigned solely to assist her while writing the training program or collecting knowledge for any purpose.

When to use a Dedicated SME:

- When the content developers are not confident that they can understand a complex or intimidating topic using the regular steps for working with client SMEs
- When your client's expert may not be available for the amount of time you need to fully understand your topic or develop your content due to the demands of their regular jobs
- When your client SME may not have time for thorough reviews of your material
- When your internal or client SMEs are in disagreement and differences in material need to be negotiated by an outside arbiter

Things to consider when hiring a dedicated SME:

- You are sure that the subject matter is incomprehensible to you without one.
- The project price supports it and the internal or external client is willing to pay for it.
- The SME for Hire works well with the client's expert.

- The Dedicated SME supports the firm's mission and fits into the culture.
- You are certain that there are not enough SMEs with enough time in the organization you are working with to help you gather and review the content.

A Dedicated SME Can Be an Ongoing Asset

A Dedicated SME for Hire can be a valuable asset in helping you create a strong product when the above mentioned conditions exist. As an added bonus, after a training contract firm has hired a SME in a specific topic area, that company has strengthened its hand in that field and can expand its offerings when similar needs arise with other customers.

As I touched on earlier, if you are a training consultancy, you may want to consider hiring a subject matter expert when you are building competency as a single topic training house. The cost and dedication to this effort is usually substantial, but if you are working in a business that is willing to pay for you to acquire this competency by paying for The Dedicated SME's time, you can yield the benefits.

12
TIPS, TOOLS, AND CHECKLISTS FOR WRANGLING EXPERTS

Every good outcome usually has some sort of plan behind it. That is true of building a great training course, designing a great golf course, or constructing the Brooklyn Bridge.

All projects, large and small, need at least a solid blueprint before you dig in. When working with an expert, he will need some guidance to make sure things run smoothly because while your SME may be an expert in a particular subject, he or she may not have project management skills. When you engage an expert in your cause, lead the effort with purpose and a plan.

Before you begin, your expert needs to know:

- Objectives and goals for the project (and perhaps some involvement in determining them)
- Information you need from them to achieve the objectives
- A process and timetable for your project

None of these items should be a surprise to him or to you.

To avoid confusion during the project or to avert derailing your project completely, start with the end in mind and then create a general map for getting there.

This chapter contains elements to consider as you put together a project plan including checklists, templates, and ideas for transferring expertise from the expert's brain to the people who need it whether they are new employees, colleagues, customers, the public, or any other audience. With that intent in mind, these are general suggestions. You may want to adapt them to your circumstance.

Subject matter expertise is employed in many ways including informing marketing efforts, professional colleagues, and the general public. It is hoped that some of these suggestions are helpful to anyone who is involved in transferring knowledge under any circumstance.

Anything worth preserving is worth preserving accurately. With that intent, here are some recommendations for working with subject matter experts to capture and preserve knowledge intact and efficiently.

The following lists and charts are segmented into two subsections:

1. The first section provides job aides to the content gatherer and developer. Its goal is to offer guidance to content professionals such as instructional designers, marketing, sales, public relations, business and industry press, and others who package information for others to consume.
2. The second section contains a few job aides to help experts who are working with content developers to ensure a smooth process and end result which reflects the intent of the expert.

Tips, Tricks, and Tools for Content Developers and Project Managers

The following recommended processes are presented in tear sheet fashion with the intent that they can be duplicated for continued use.

Tear Sheet #1: Project Plan Checklist

I have considered:

- Limitations of time, funding, and personnel as I create schedules and commit resources
- Organization of the project in numbered steps with clear milestones
- Realistic development timelines for myself and others involved
- Adequate time for review cycles
- All the stakeholders and sponsors that must sign off and approve content including those funding the project
- Subject matter expert(s) who is/are critical to the project
- Backup resources for all critical experts
- Clear lines of responsibility and authority for everyone on the project
- Required regulatory or compliance guidelines and corporate best practices

List project funders and sponsors with signoff authority

_____

_____

_____

_____

_____

_____

_____

_____

List special considerations for this project

_____

_____

_____

_____

_____

_____

_____

_____

Tear Sheet #2: Write a Project Charter

A project charter establishes the need and the permission for your work. Whenever you run into a question about direction or need for authority, this should be your go-to document.

Purpose of the Charter

The project charter defines the scope, objectives, and overall approach for the work to be completed. It is a critical element in initiating, planning, executing, controlling, and assessing the project. It is an initial single point of reference on the project for project goals and objectives, scope, estimates, roles and responsibilities, and timelines. In addition, it serves as a contract between the project team and the project sponsors, stating what will be delivered according to the agreed upon budget, time constraints, risks, resources, and standards.

About the Client

Describes the business and mission.

Project Overview

Describes the topic(s) of the project and the audiences who are the targets of the information.

Project Goals

Describes the goals of the project and how they tie to business objectives.

Expected Outcomes

Lists the desired outcomes of the project, including its effects on employees, customers, vendors, investors or any other stakeholders, and its intended effect on business results.

Content

Describes the topics and length of the project to be developed.

Audience

Lists those who will consume the information and categories of stakeholders who will be impacted.

Deliverable Requirements

Lists the components including software to be developed or used in achieving the deliverable (i.e., Articulate®, PowerPoint®, facilitator's guide, mentoring guide, job aides, posters, marketing materials, articles, etc.)

Assessment and Evaluation

Describes the type of assessments to be included, how effectiveness will be measured and acknowledged, and how and when the project outcomes will be evaluated.

Upfront Planning, Ongoing Project Management, and Project Schedule

Create a project plan using a program such as MS Project, Smartsheet, Unfuddle, Excel or create one of your own. New and easy to use project management and team communication software continues to come to market, so check out one that works best in your situation. It does not matter which program you use; it only matters that you have a common platform that can be shared among team members. A detailed project plan will include milestones for information gathering, review cycles, and signoffs. It may include provisions for alpha, beta, and final versions.

Assumptions

Describes any specific, unusual, or mandatory requirements to be considered in the design, development, delivery, and evaluation of the program or project.

Project Alerts

Project alerts are documented in the project plan. Issues that require immediate attention should be addressed with the project manager and project sponsor. The guidelines for priority criteria should be used to determine issue priority.

Priority Criteria

1. High priority/critical path issue requires immediate follow-up and resolution
2. Medium priority issue requires follow-up before completion of next project milestone
3. Low priority issue is to be resolved prior to project completion
4. Closed issue

Project Style Guidelines

Describes the branding of materials and style guidelines for written and graphic content, etc.

Tear Sheet #3: Project Charter Checklist

Scope

Define the content parameters – Topic, estimate hours, budget, deadline, and deliverables

_____

_____

Goal – What business goal is achieved

_____

_____

Objective – What performance or identifiable end result is achieved

_____

_____

- The funder or paying client's business or mission

_____

- Project overview – Topic(s) to be trained or addressed

_____

_____

- Project goals – How goals relate to business objectives

_____

_____

_____

- Expected outcome(s) – What people will be able to do, the effect they will have on performance of the organization, and its business outcomes

_____

_____

_____

- Content – Topics and length in time/pages

_____

_____

_____

_____

- Audience – The people who are the intended recipients of this information

_____

_____

- Technical requirements – Software, hardware, and other materials needed to complete the project (specify vendors and specific product names if necessary)

_____

_____

_____

_____

- Assessment and evaluation – Types and frequency of assessments and evaluations to determine if you are hitting your
  time, budget, goals, and objectives

- Project management – Project management plan with milestones to track progress, hours, budget, and identify platform
  (project management software)

- Assumptions – Specific, unusual, or mandatory requirements to
  be considered in the design, development, delivery, or evaluation

---

- Project alert status – Issues that require immediate attention and must be addressed by the project manager or project
  sponsors
  1. High priority/critical- path issue requires immediate
     follow-up and resolution
  2. Medium priority issue requires follow-up before comple-
     tion of next project milestone
  3. Low priority issue is to be resolved prior to project
     completion
  4. Closed issue

• Style guidelines – Branding of materials, required formatting, or inclusion of regulatory or compliance documents

Tear Sheet #4: Checklist for Gathering and Organizing
Information from Your Subject Matter Experts

This quick checklist will help you think about what to consider when
you are doing your information gathering with your expert.

Conduct a Well Planned Interview

- Schedule interviews at least two weeks in advance.
- Plan questions before the interview to get the most information.
- Stay on track and monitor your time.
- Take notes, record conversations, and take photos.
- Create diagrams or flow charts if appropriate.
- Allow time and structure the interview to allow for unanticipated information.
- Balance "go with the flow" and "control."
- Schedule a follow-up meeting and signoff.
- End on time.

Be a Project Manager

- Manage the communications, meetings, and people involved.
- Respect their time.
- Make sure all parties agree to a schedule for meetings.
- Keep meetings focused and brief.
- Have a schedule for meetings, review cycles, and signoffs.
- Include the SME, instructional designers, graphic designers, editors, and any other stakeholders in signoffs.
- Remember that you are managing corporate resources, so respect people's time.

Create a Schedule and Plan

- Determine the best days, times, and places.
- Determine the meeting length.
- Include what you will collect and how you will review, confirm, or authorize it.
- Ask for "pre-work" before interviews – slides, articles, reports, and charts.
- Build in cycle time for comments, corrections, and revisions.

Tear Sheet #5: Common Sense Guidelines for Project Managers

Good leadership and project management principles will help you manage the process of content collection between a content developer and the SME and with anyone else on the team who is involved in the process of knowledge capture and transfer.

Whether you are the content developer in a dual role also acting as the PM, or if you are solely engaged as the PM, here are a few common sense but important guidelines for project management to control risk when working with subject matter experts:

- **Define the human resources**. Make sure you have assigned the correct SMEs, training designers, content developers, or other essential knowledge gathering members to the project.
- **Have a toolkit of templates** for collecting, organizing, and reviewing content. Make sure your team has them, understands them, and uses them, although expect them to modify these templates to meet the needs of the project.
- **Schedule milestones** and notify all team members about their deadlines.
- **Check in with the writer or instructional designer** to make sure she is getting what she needs from her SME.
- **If there appears to be content or deadline problems, check in with the expert** to make sure she is able to provide what is needed, can stay on schedule, and is comfortable with the work product being created.
- **Schedule regular updates** from the PM outlining progress to everyone involved in the process. Weekly updates are recommended, more frequently if the project is urgent and less frequently as the project winds down.
- **Make sure everyone is clear** about their levels of responsibility and authority.

Tear Sheet #6: Roles and Responsibilities Chart

List the names of the people who are responsible for each part of the project. Adjust role names to reflect your culture.

ROLE	PERSON(S)
Executive Sponsor/Owner	
Senior Consultant/Firm	
Project Manager	
Subject Matter Expert(s)	
Backup Subject Matter Expert(s)	
Content Developer/Instructional Designer(s)	
Editor/QA (s)	
Graphic Designer/Firm	
Client Relationship Manager	
Other	
Other	

Tear Sheet #7: Subject Matter Expert Contact List

SUBJECT MATTER EXPERT CONTACT LIST

Job Number:

Job Title:

Company:

Client (who is paying)/Title:

Client Phone, Email:

Contract Start Date:

Description of Work:

Lead Developer:

CONTACT/SME NAME	DEPARTMENT/ TITLE/TOPIC	PHONE NUMBER	EMAIL	AVAILABILITY (BEST TIMES, DAYS, WEEKS)

Tear Sheet #8: Content Gathering Session Cover Sheet

Ideally, content gathering sessions are no longer than 2 hours. Using a cover sheet like this one ensures that the meeting and its contents stay on track and are documented and approved. In most complicated programs, more than one session is needed. The key to a successful interview is to read any preparatory materials provided by the SME before the session. If no preparatory materials are provided, the content developer should do some research on the topic to prepare good questions.

The importance of starting with a list of prepared questions cannot be overemphasized. As a rule, a prepared question list should start with establishing some very basic information such as spelling the name and title of the SME correctly, noting the time and date of the interview, and asking a few broad questions to begin the conversation. Those questions will have several branches of progressive detail. Leave time for asking more questions in response to the expert's answers. In general, a great interview gathers all the essential information identified in your interview plan and is flexible enough to pursue the unexpected – very important pieces of information gleaned through the interview process. When gathering information for training particularly, the interviewer and interviewee will continue to check their questions and answers against the predetermined learning objectives for the course during the interview to be sure they are staying on track. You can use a Content Gathering Session Cover Sheet like the one that follows to track your interviews.

Content Gathering Session Cover Sheet

PROJECT NAME

Content Developer/Instructional Designer
Subject Matter Expert
Date/Time of Interview
Oral Interview: (note time/length/recording)
Interview Transcription Approved by SME
List of Prepared Questions Attached
Receipt of Information
Materials: (list PPTs, reports, web links, etc.)
- Provided before interview
- Provided during interview
- To be provided after the interview
Location of physical file and/or electronic file for client assets (i.e., all materials provided to create the training program)

Tear Sheet #9: Standard Interview Questions

The following questions are suggestions for information you should consider when you talk to your subject matter expert. They are broadly worded so you can adapt the questions to your situation.

Consider these types of questions when you talk to an expert. Ask about:

1. Length of career, education, history with company or field
2. Details of studies or techniques provided
3. Ways this may differ from current knowledge, skills, and attitudes
4. Any simple steps, shortcuts, or easy ways to remember this information
5. Ways this information can be applied immediately
6. Any warnings or special care instructions
7. Variations or exceptions to the knowledge provided
8. When and where to apply the knowledge
9. Types of exercises or practice to reinforce the knowledge
10. Any anticipated changes in this knowledge, field, and, technique
11. "Is there anything I did not ask you that you think should be included?"
12. Date and time of the next interview or check review schedule for materials created

Tear Sheet #10: Expert Interview Checklist

- Check the spelling of the name; check title and credentials.
- Note the date (day/month/year) and time of the interview.
- Get permission to record an audio or a video.
- Note the format of recording.
- Get the transcript and/or notes checked by the interviewer and expert.
- List prepared questions (see Standard Interview Questions).
- List documents and supplementary material – slides, websites, journal articles, books, recordings, etc. Note the dates received.

_____

_____

_____

- Create physical and/or electronic files for all materials received.
- Create physical and/or electronic files for all materials created.

Tear Sheet #11: Review Cycle Capture Log

When you are working with experts, you need to check that you have correctly captured and interpreted the material. You may find when you are working with a true expert, he or she is in a field that has a language all its own. Even an innocent word used incorrectly could be misinterpreted in certain disciplines, so although you may be confident that you have captured everything accurately and an editor has approved your content, make sure the expert gets another look at what you have created.

If you have scheduled a review as part of the project plan, the expert will be expecting to check your work. Often, you will have more than one reviewer: an editor for style and grammar, an expert or several to check accuracy of information, an executive to check for adherence to company policies, a regulatory or compliance agent for adherence to rules and regulations, and so on.

The following spreadsheet is a sample snapshot of the kind of document you can create that can help track the reviewers as well as the actions taken to resolve any issues they identify. You can use this idea and modify it with your own language and project specifications.

During a review cycle, be sure the following types of questions are addressed (Figure 12.1):

- Does the content cover the business goals?
- Does the content address the business goals in a way that helps the intended audience meet outcomes?
- Would a content consumer (new employee, customer, general public, etc.) be able to follow and understand the material?
- Do all the steps and supporting information adequately explain the processes or topic covered?
- Have you checked all client specific information, terms, forms, systems, processes, or report names for accuracy?
- Could any part of the materials use further explanation to increase clarity beyond that which is covered?
- Do your corrections precisely indicate what changes are needed, leaving no room for misinterpretation by content developers or others involved in delivering the project?

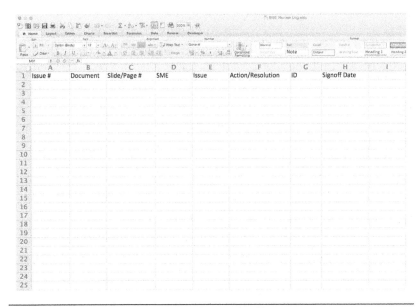

Figure 12.1   Review cycle log – sample worksheet in Excel®

Tear Sheet #12: SME Acknowledgement of Review

I understand that the accuracy of the attached documents is the responsibility of client's/department's employees. By signing below, I am verifying that I have thoroughly read the document for context, detail, and accuracy. To the best of my knowledge, the document is correct except where noted.

#	DOCUMENT TITLE	1ST DRAFT APPROVAL SME		FINAL APPROVAL SME		FINAL APPROVAL TEAM LEADER/ PROJECT MANAGER		FINAL APPROVAL DIRECTOR	
1		Initials	Date	Initials	Date	Initials	Date	Initials	Date
2									
3									

Tear Sheet #13: Follow-Up and Wrap-Up Signoffs

When a project is complete, make sure you have the approval and signoff of all the experts, reviewers, and people with lines of authority to the project. Their signatures validate the content and may even be necessary to have the budget appropriation or final payment approved.

Earlier you listed stakeholders, including project owners with responsibility, accountability, and budget authority in your project charter. Those are the signatures you need on this document. You can modify the Signoff Sheet below to designate the names and roles of people who may have emerged as ultimately responsible for the work product during the course of the project.

I APPROVE THE FINAL DRAFT OF THE MATERIALS. SIGNATURE	DATE RECEIVED	CHECK BOX TO INDICATE APPROVAL
Subject Matter Expert		
Team Lead/Manager		
Director/Client		
Project Manager		
Other Stakeholder(s)		

Tear Sheet #14: Project Evaluation Checklist

The unexamined life is not worth living

Greek philosopher Plato circa 400 B.C.

Plato got it right. By extension, the unexamined project is a lost opportunity to learn something valuable about your people, processes, and organizational culture. Whether your project hit every goal on time and within budget and the product is stellar or if you missed most of your major milestones and are left with a half-baked result, you will benefit from all your hard work when you stop to review the project afterwards.

First, make sure you celebrate completion and acknowledge the hard work that went into achieving it.

Next, conduct an After Action Review. Reviewing the actions and results of a project is part of winding down, getting resolution, learning, and moving on.

After a project is completed, set aside an hour with the team to review the highlights and figure out what worked, what did not, and what you can learn from the experience. A good After Action Review is short and simple and focuses on the main themes, successes, and opportunities for improvement.

A successful After Action Review will:

- Focus directly on the intended goals, tasks, and outcomes
- Attempt to discover what actually happened and why
- Encourage participants to discuss important lessons learned
- Capture process improvements for future projects
- Applaud the team's successes

An After Action Review does not:

- Judge success or failure
- Assign blame to anyone

Tear Sheet #15: After Action Review Template

WHAT WERE OUR INTENDED RESULTS?	WHAT WERE OUR ACTUAL RESULTS?	WHAT CAUSED OUR RESULTS?

WHAT WORKED WELL THAT WE WILL DO AGAIN NEXT TIME?

WHAT WILL WE DO DIFFERENTLY NEXT TIME?

Tips, Tricks, and Tools for Subject Matter Experts

It is said that God helps those who help themselves. The content developer's corollary might well be that experts help content developers who help them do their jobs well.

Since you have already engaged the subject matter expert in your cause to capture his or her knowledge intact to deliver it to others and spread the word, give your expert a little guidance before you start. These two tear sheets will help your expert know what to expect and how to best achieve knowledge transfer as efficiently as possible.

Share the two following lists of guidelines and tips with your SME to make the process smoother for both of you.

SME Tear Sheet #1: Process Tips for the Expert Content Contributor

Although the content creator is responsible for the correct capture of your knowledge, you can make contributions to a successful project by keeping a few simple tips in mind.

1. **Organization** – If the steps or flow of the content the creator has outlined for you do not make sense, put them in a logical sequence. Nobody understands the context of the material better than you and that includes the content developer.

2. **Timeliness** – Be available for interviews and do reviews on time. Your content development partner faces deadline pressures from people like editors and designers whose schedules depend on yours.

3. **Scheduling Conflicts** – Anticipate and avoid scheduling conflicts. This seems obvious, but you will find that sometimes your regular work may directly conflict with meeting your SME obligation. If you are in a job where this can occur, plan for this contingency. For example, ask the content creator if you can work ahead on your deadline for reviews, comments, and signoffs. The content developer, and probably also a graphic designer, computer programmer, project manager, and an editor – at the very least – have their work schedules dependent upon your deadline too. Time is money all the way around. While the time and money associated with the cost of developing the training program may not be obvious, other people's deadlines and budgets are affected by your ability to fit this obligation into your schedule. Sometimes the content creator is working on competing projects and may not have the flexibility to adjust to last minute scheduling changes.

4. **Accuracy** – Provide the information requested and double check to make sure it is correct when you get drafts of the program (and yes, you may receive more than one.) This seems simple enough and may even seem insulting to mention, but it would not be here if failure to check information did not happen. Your content creator is not the expert; that is why he or she needs you to make sure it is right.

5. **Signoffs** – Sign off at pre-agreed checkpoints and make sure you have checked the accuracy of the information when you do. If you are working with a contract content developer from outside your company, there is probably a contract in place between the consulting organization and your company that makes your company responsible for content after you affix your signature to it. If you sign off on incorrect information, it will cost your company when the project goes into overruns for corrections or scope creep. Internally, your signoff means the program is going to be finalized, packaged, and used by learners who are your coworkers. Your signoff not only is the hallmark of your credibility, but it affects the performance of other people in your organization for years to come.

6. **Blind Spots** – We all have them. Frequently, we develop blind spots as a result of our success; failures are more likely to call us up short and require us to be careful and thorough. Because you are the SME, let us assume you have met with a lot of success in your life; that makes you vulnerable to blind spots. Think through the eyes of a novice when you are explaining details to your content creator. He has not walked a mile in your shoes so make clear each stone along the path.

SME Tear Sheet #2: Top 10 Tips for Experts:
How to Provide Great Information

1. Think of the content creator as a court reporter. He or she will take note of everything you say and will later use those notes to create content for a training asset, article, sales, or marketing program.

2. Keep in mind that procedures and knowledge are often being written for new hires or complete novices, not seasoned experts. Remember that a new hire needs to know every single step in a procedure and needs explanations of complex concepts. For example, pressing the "enter" key after an action might seem like old hat to you, but would a new hire know to do it?

3. In addition to giving the *whats*, remember to give the *whos, whens and whys*. When you're giving instructions for completing a specific action, tell the content creator *who* the action will affect, *when* the action will take place in relation to the entire process, and *why* the action needs to be taken. Context is critical to understanding.

4. When creating introductory material for individual sections of new information, aim for the overall picture first. Think of the best way to describe the reason for the section to a neophyte. Again, look at the *who, when* and *why*, in addition to the *what*.

    Poor Introduction: "The following procedures will allow you to set up a Basic Control Account."

    Why is this poor? This sentence only describes *what* the learner is expected to know.

    Good Introduction: Before clients can be enrolled in the Corporate Travel program, a Basic Control Account (BCA) needs to be established. BCA is the lowest level of a company's corporate account hierarchy structure. All clients fall under a BCA. The following are steps for setting up a Basic Control Account. When the BCA is set up, you can enroll individual clients.

    Why is this good? The paragraph describes *what* the learner is expected to do, *when* he is expected to do it, *who* is affected and *why* they are performing the task.

5. Remember that the content creator only knows what you have told him. Consider yourself the information expert and the developer as the novice. Inaccurate procedures arise when a content developer attempts to interpret ideas or fill in missing links of information. To avoid misinterpretation, think through the wording of a step in your head first and then say it aloud. If you have doubts about your wording, jot it down on paper and say it out loud to yourself. Before continuing to the next step, be sure to ask the content developer, "Did you get that down?"

6. When explaining complex information, stick to the main idea. Avoid extraneous information that does not pertain to the specific section you are documenting. When you are an expert, it may be difficult to determine what is extraneous to someone unfamiliar with your work so you may draw a diagram with a main idea and note its direct descendants or secondary ideas. Keep your information to the main branch and its direct descendants as much as possible. Stay close to the main path. If a concept becomes too complex, do not be afraid to break concepts or procedures into multiple sections to make the resultant explanation more user friendly. For example, a good rule is to limit procedure steps to about 10. A procedure may have 20 steps, but make that the exception, not the rule. If the number of steps or secondary ideas become excessive, break the process or concept into smaller chunks. The following diagram may help you visualize the way to share complex thoughts with a content creator (Figure 12.2).

7. While shortcuts are advantageous to someone who has worked in a field for a while, they are usually confusing to a new person. Consider providing background or giving *all* the steps to a procedure when you are with a content developer. Before giving information, ask yourself, "Is this best practice?"

8. When you make a change while reviewing a document, note your change directly on the page next to the information you are correcting whether using a review function in an electronic document or affixing a sticky note to a hard copy. Be clear about the change. Try to avoid ambiguous statements such as, "No! This step needs rework." or "More information

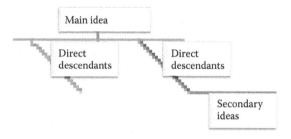

Figure 12.2 Branching diagram for main and direct descendant ideas

needed here." Instead, supply specific information so the corrections can be easily made without coming back to you for a second review process. Try to use statements such as, "Add direction after step 3: Move the cursor to the next line before proceeding."

9. Before the end of your content gathering session, take the time to review the information you discussed. The goal is to document the procedures and concepts accurately the first time. Feel free to ask the content creator to read your information back to you. As you are listening, pretend the procedure is totally new to you and imagine performing the steps or using the information as you hear it without any additional information.

10. Whenever possible, provide hard copy documentation of your information. For example, if you are working with software, provide screen prints both blank and completed for reference with visible drop down menus. If you are referencing an article you have written, provide the article. If you have a slide presentation that you have delivered on the topic, provide it. You may have charts, graphics, and sources in those materials that can be used in the materials for a training program or marketing and sales materials.

13

EXPERTS OF THE FUTURE

Dueling Experts: When You Must Decide

Sometimes different experts have differing perspectives. Anyone capturing knowledge for preservation may encounter the issue of what to do when competing experts tell different stories or, most troubling, when agendas among stakeholders obscure factual information.

The answer is when you are writing training, sales, marketing, or public relations materials for a client, the stakeholder paying the bill gets the last say. It is *his* company and *his* money; it is not your call to decide what gets captured and preserved as official knowledge within *his* organization. Of course, some knowledge is an undisputed matter of science or math and you cannot undo the realities of gravity or 1 + 1. But in any matter open to interpretation, when you are writing for a client it is the payer's perspective that wins in a matter open to expert opinion.

However, as we have discussed many times throughout this book, not all knowledge preservation falls under corporate training, sales, or marketing. People capture knowledge for many reasons and people also have many reasons for obscuring information.

Which leads in a somewhat circuitous way to discuss a very sensitive topic: whether to manipulate evidence of history to bend to the will of those in power or, if a different standard applies, to preserve the knowledge of human history.

Let us face it. Human history demonstrates that not all knowledge is savory.

A Societal Application: When Passions Are Inflamed, Reason Flees

Human history is awash with stories of armed conquests, atrocities and man's inhumanity to man. The evidence remains intact at the

Colosseum in Rome, at the crematoria that stand as testament to the horrors of WWII Nazi death camps, and yes, in the bone-laden killing fields around the world where despots wreaked death on millions of people in the name of some ideology. Those horrible monuments stand as silent screams that those events occurred. Such it is in the United States where Americans, too, have some violent and inhumane history we do not want to repeat. When passions are inflamed, reason flees. We need to be reminded where we have been so we can avoid retreading that bloody ground.

As vendors of accuracy (ah, a new meme!), those who are tasked with recording knowledge and information for preservation are called on to record it all. Just the way it happened. To the best of their ability. Representing all points of view and all versions of events. That way we can reproduce what works and avoid what does not work in the future. We can do more of the right thing and less of the wrong thing. Earlier, I discussed Henry Ford's statement that he fired the experts because they knew all the ways things could not be done. While we want to put new, fresh minds to work on innovation, it is a good idea to keep the old heads around to tell you where the landmines are. So it is with preservation of historical fact.

Important books in our literature like *Fahrenheit 451 by Ray Bradbury* and *Animal Farm by George Orwell* warn of the perils of obscuring or rewriting history. People with agendas who burn books are in a position to tell a new, albeit, inaccurate and incomplete story. As we are told, those who do not know history are destined to repeat it. Despotic rulers and invading armies destroy the histories and culture of the places they conquer so the vanquished cannot retrace either their roots to preserve their strengths or remember their tragedies. The victors write the history books. To have a just, whole, and open society, people need to have an accurate knowledge of all that has gone before – the good and the horrific.

By destroying or masking terrible truths, we doom ourselves to repeat them – and to be controlled by people who want to rewrite history for their own ends. Because we have ample evidence of the sordid underbelly of the monsters in history, we know what happens after the books are burned and history is obscured. Without those reminders, we are vulnerable to bad information and bad outcomes.

In writing proprietary material for a privately held company, the stakeholder with the checkbook has the last word on content. As for the story of human history, I invite you to consider that each individual is an equal stakeholder in society so we need the most complete story we can assemble for a 360° view of reality. History tells us and literature warns us to beware of any group that wants to control the historical narrative.

When content developers are tasked with preserving sensitive information that has significance beyond a single company, fidelity to accuracy carries a weightier responsibility to the truth.

Sunlight is a disinfectant. Let events stand as their own witnesses.

Managing Tomorrow's Experts: Are Traditional Experts and NextGen Experts Different?

Our focus has been retiring experts. Considering the rapid acquisition of knowledge in the last century, we cannot end our discussion on preserving expert knowledge without turning our attention to the next chapter of knowledge, the experts of tomorrow. Unlike their more linear, older counterparts, the experts of tomorrow will drive individual and corporate knowledge with global, instantaneous proliferation of information.

Let us look at some contrast.

1950s: The astrophysicist of yesteryear studied in relative isolation, probably in an exclusive school gleaning formulae from weighty tomes speaking almost exclusively among (usually) his limited universe of peers. Very few outside his esoteric circle understood or related to his comprehension of relativity.

Today: The astrophysicist delivers online classes from MIT widely available on MOOC platforms watched by your curious and precocious 12-year-old. Your son or daughter jumps on social media to post a cool link to the lecture. Friends "like" it or comment that he or she is a nerd or a rocket scientist or give your child some other social nod of approval. The NextGen astrophysicist moves effortlessly in the flow of like minds.

Two radically different cultural and educational milieu a half century apart are going to produce two very different types of experts. An experience of isolation and exception versus an experience of community and commonality will affect the expert's personality, as well as how they see themselves, how they see their place in the world, and how they share what they know.

A Traditional Expert will carry the experience all his life of being exceptional, being misunderstood, and being isolated from the mainstream. A NextGen Expert swims in the social flow connecting easily with like-minded peers from the U.S., Russia, China, Britain, and Germany.

Of course, not all experts are astrophysicists. The above example is extreme. Your experts will come from all backgrounds and fields of study. Your Traditional Expert may be the nurse who has been there for 30 years, the machinist who has run that lathe since he graduated from high school, or the chemist in your lab who has not looked up from his beaker since Reagan left office. All of them grew up in the same environment of relative isolation and exclusivity in their domain. That is, relative to the widely available, global, and instantaneous communication and education of the NextGen of experts who are carrying forward the torch of knowledge in their fields on the Internet.

As we mentioned earlier, due to the instantaneous communication and rapid proliferation of ideas, it is estimated that knowledge now doubles about every 12 months. That, too, changes the nature of experts because no expert remains one for very long.

These changes have implications for learning, teaching, and working styles that impact the way you collect and transfer expertise in your own organization.

Expect a few things from NextGen Experts:

- Knowledge is widely dispersed, and they are open and generous with their knowledge.
- What they know is openly explained and shared widely.
- Expertise is not exclusive.
- Knowledge not widely shared is not valuable.
- Transfer of knowledge is open sourced and curated.
- Learning is tailored to the task, the learner, and the environment in which they apply it.

Consider the differences between the Traditional Expert and the NextGen Expert when you create your knowledge management plan going forward. As you look at how to structure interactions with NextGen Experts, the following table contrasts knowledge acquisition and transfer styles. Consider that you may not have to create a structured knowledge transfer plan at all – in the traditional sense. NextGen Experts are natural sharers and learners, a circumstance that may make the traditional training role obsolete.

Figure 13.1 compares the mindset of the Traditional Expert versus that of the NextGen Expert towards knowledge acquisition, capture, and transfer. Yes, what a difference a generation makes!

Will Artificial Intelligence Make Your Experts Extinct?

Before we leave, consider whether the expert of the future is necessary– or human – or relevant – in light of the rapid advances in artificial intelligence.

Traditional Expert	NextGen Expert
Exclusive knowledge	Widely available knowledge
Assumes your ignorance	Assumes your interest
Professional isolation	Professional community
Sharing is exclusive	Sharing is commonplace
Knowledge transfer is restricted and expensive	Knowledge transfer is open and demonetized
Information is structured within frameworks	Information flows freely and is redefined continuously
Learning happens in classrooms, when ordered	Learning happens all the time, as needed
The right way is static	The right way changes with conditions and new information
Topic defines teaching method	Student-centered learning methods
Apprenticeships for the young	Lifelong learning

Figure 13.1   Traditional vs. NextGen Expert approaches to knowledge sharing

Traditional employees were schooled in a linear and proprietary culture. Your Traditional employees often are people with a static mindset who worry about capturing current internal expertise for future business growth. After all, what is has always been and will always be, or so traditional thinking goes.

This static mindset extends to workers caught in a traditional manufacturing or service provider paradigm who are concerned they will be replaced by robots. Experience justifies their concern. It is a legitimate expectation because it happens every day. Business owners are always looking for ways to do things more consistently, efficiently, and cheaply and robotics often solves that problem. However, when you replace humans, you also introduce the problem of displaced workers. The social implications are astounding so we will not go there in this book; that is the subject for many other books in other disciplines outside knowledge management.

However, it is in our purview to consider two questions as the uptake of robots and artificial intelligence (AI) affects capturing corporate expertise:

1. If you plan to "hire" robots to do the jobs of humans, you may conclude you do not need to capture human knowledge. Human skills are so "Encyclopedia Britannica" and robots are so "search engine". Those companies looking toward the future are living in the gap, waiting for the next wave of industrialization that antiquates their current business model and their need for training humans.

2. If you eliminate human workers, how do you pay robots? As I thought about traditional accounting methods, I figured robots are a capital expense like buildings and machinery, but believe it or not, economists are now working out a way to pay for and tax the "labor" of robots which puts them in the category of "worker". AI robots may be your experts of the future. This is where cryptocurrency comes in. You can "pay" robots in cryptocurrency. It is right there in the book *Digital Gold* on page 294.

Like many [Silicon] Valley firms, Andreesen's was thinking about intelligent robots, and Bitcoin seemed like a perfect medium of exchange for two machines that needed to pay each other for services. – Digital Gold: Bitcoin and the Inside Story of the Misfits and Millionaires Trying to Reinvent Money.

Nathaniel Popper, HarperCollins, *New York, 2015*

Breathe.

A lot of the forward thinkers who are instituting new systems of work, the economy, the social structure, and so on are pondering these questions. If they succeed in fully automating work, theoretically, it frees the rest of us to be creative and pursue our passions while being supported by a basic income supplied – I assume – by the robots' productivity.

Seriously, people are having these discussions right now. You may have heard Facebook founder Mark Zuckerberg call for Universal Basic Income (UBI) in his 2017 Harvard Commencement address.[*] It's a real thing. The robots work, get paid in cryptocurrency, are potentially taxed on their labor and citizens get paid from the labor of robots to take macramé classes.

A consultant from Australia, Steve Hutson, Director of Hutson Group [Automation Revolution],[†] spends part of his time grappling with questions about the future of the human knowledge worker. He sees many changes ahead in the deployment and use of artificial intelligence and its effect on the value of human expertise. Hutson believes that some functions of human intelligence that are impacted by the rather esoteric concepts of intuition and spirituality are not easily replicable by AI.

In an interview in August 2017, he said:

"I'm a technologist, integrator and socio-technology observer [sic] (the study of human interaction and behavoir [sic]with technology at an indivual, [sic] organisational and gobals [sic] levels); all I do do[sic] is simply impliment [sic] my findings in business and educate others to do the same thing . . .

---

[*] Accessed September 27, 2017 at http://money.cnn.com/2017/05/26/news/economy/mark-zuckerberg-universal-basic-income/index.html.

[†] Email August 10, 2017. Automation Revolution, website accessed August 10, 2017 at https://www.hutsongroup.com.au/.

". . .my services are not for everybody as it tends to break most of the common rules we 'are lead [sic] to believe' – open minded poeple [sic] that is [sic] open to 'new information' are always a pleasure to work with. In short, what we define as human expert knowledge today could one day be considered obsolete and this may be a gradual thing as various, particular skills are replaced over a long time period. For example, the current AI used in scanning for cancer and other related abnormalities already is used today [in incidences when] a highly qualified doctor may not pick [it] up.

"However, all this does is redefine 'human expertise.' There is a level of self-awareness and ability to accept and allow new information to enter one's thoughts that probably will never be replaced. Dreaming and waking up from a dream where answers to solutions have come to you in the middle of night is only one example. Meditation is another [example] of where new information can come from. Until AI has the ability to achieve this level of awareness, it probably won't make human expertise obsolete [but] only redefine it …

"We are already well moving towards accepting [intuitive and spiritual] new information as a global movement and implementing [this type of] information into professional offerings. It is still a widely [considered] a voodoo thing by the majority and often not considered mainstream. There are no official qualifications for somebody that successfully operates on gut feelings in a profession; these people will be the last to be replaced - if at all. I don't believe it to be possible for humans to create an AI that can simulate awareness and implement it until we have at least understood awareness at such level it can be created by man. AI will play a big role in years to come but may get to a point where it gets stuck for a very long time, and when we do we will need human expertise to challenge the problems [we face] …

"Of course, we already have some 'useful' AI at very specialized levels and this sector will grow until we hit that point, when problems need to be solved by thinking outside of the box. And just maybe we need this to happen to then acknowledge [human] awareness at the higher level to become a mainstream and accepted form of expertise."

To Hutson's point about the current uses of AI to supplement or replace human judgment is this article from MobiHealthNews on

August 8, 2017. In *Teenage Team Develops AI to Screen for Diabetic Neuropathy* by Jeff Lagasse*, we learn that a high school student developed a smartphone application and 3D printed lens that allow patients to self-screen for diabetic retinopathy. She used a machine learning architecture called a convolutional neural network – like photos – to scan for patterns leveraging the ability of artificial intelligence to classify images. Tested against the diagnostic ability of five ophthalmologists, the smartphone app was just as reliable as the human doctors.

The question that remains is whether AI's diagnostic accuracy for this type of utilization will translate to making human judgment obsolete over time. If Hutson is correct, the unquantifiable qualities of human intelligence will be difficult, if not impossible, to replicate. It may be our superconscious beyond the measurement of machines that gives human experts an edge over their technology replacements.

Those who study expertise have determined that the average expert makes as many as 50,000 simultaneous judgments when they are assessing a situation in his or her field, and Hutson postulates it is this intuitive and indefinable knowledge application that will remain the purview of the human expert.

I Do Not Digress

You may think I digress from our regularly scheduled topic of capturing and retaining your corporate subject matter expertise. This actually is not a digression at all. This discussion is essential to our topic of whether human knowledge is important, essential, needs to be captured and carried on – or really has any value at all – in light of the rapid progress in robots and artificial intelligence. For those of us who follow developments in the training world, you know that we are learning how to train robots. Research is making the leap so that

---

* Accessed on August 8, 2017 at http://www.mobihealthnews.com/content/teenage-team-develops-ai-system-screen-diabetic-retinopathy?mkt_tok=eyJpIjoiTlRJMk56 RTBNek5qTURJdyIsInQiOiJuQnJ6QmF2SlpQUDVsU1FNTVwvTzRoVHVMS UVacHZwNjl2QWFxVDRqUU9xTGdLeXFhWkE0OVM5VFplQTVMMTN TZkV6XC9pMDVyV2trVXRHZmxHTlhETWhGXC9ZK1RWNHRYcUhCZ HRuZCslXC83bEYyXC9FYzJWS2dUOHMwdHVqNTZEelBNIn0%3D.

robots can now acquire learning that builds on prior knowledge – you know, the same way we silly old humans learn.

If you believe the future is here, you are right. If you believe you still have to operate in the present, you are also right.

For those of us still living in the pre-AI world before we all receive a Universal Basic Income, we need to continue to contend with the issues of human knowledge capture, retention, and transfer between generations of workers for the ongoing success of your enterprise.

Making a Plan to Retain Human Knowledge
Until the Robots Take Over

If your experts flee to retirement or leave your organization for any other reason, you are still vulnerable to losing their valuable knowledge, skills. and attitudes to fulfill your mission effectively, efficiently and in a cost responsible way today.

What are you doing right now to make sure you keep your expertise under your roof even if your experts leave?

Here is what we can do today to help you raise awareness about these issues in your organization:

- Speak to your organization's decision makers to help them analyze their risk of losing valuable expertise.
- Explore which workshops can help you dissect your organization for areas where you are vulnerable to losing your critical experts.
- Help identify and work with individual experts in your organization.

Think about it.

Until the robots take over, you still need a plan!

Bibliography

5 Generations – 1 Workplace: Maximizing the Potential of a Generational Shift. Glaser L. July 9, 2014. 2014 Mid America Labor-Management Conference. U.S. Federal Mediation & Conciliation Service.

7 Ways Young Leaders Succeed With Elders. Rockwell D. August 14, 2016. Accessed September 26, 2017 at https://leadershipfreak.wordpress.com/2016/08/14/7-ways-young-leaders-succeed-with-elders/.

Abundance: The Future Is Better Than You Think. Diamandis P., Kotler S. 2012. Simon & Schuster. New York, NY.

The Attacker's Advantage. Charan R. 2015. PublicAffairs. New York, NY.

Bold: How to Go Big, Create Wealth and Impact the World. Diamandis P., Kotler S. 2015. Simon & Schuster. New York, NY.

Deep Time: How Humanity Communicates Across Millenia. Benford G. 1996. University of California Press. Oakland, CA.

Digital Gold: Bitcoin and the Inside Story of the Misfits and Millionaires Trying to Reinvent Money. Popper N. 2015. HarperCollins. New York, NY.

The Experts in Your Midst. Prietula M.J., Simon H.A. *Harvard Business Review*. January–February 1989. Accessed March 20, 2018 at https://hbr.org/1989/01/the-experts-in-your-midst.

Finding Your SMEs: Capturing Knowledge from Retiring Subject Matter Experts in Your Organization Before They Leave. Salvatore P. 2016. Self-Published CreateSpace. Bethlehem, PA.

Future Shock. Toffler A. 1970. Random House. New York, NY.

The Implications of Organizational Forgetting. Lawrence T. *Training Industry Magazine*. Summer 2014.

The Law of Accelerating Returns. Kurzweil R. March 7, 2001. Essays. Kurzweil Accelerating Intelligence. Accessed September 2, 2017 at http://www.kurzweilai.net/the-law-of-accelerating-returns.

Learning Environments by Design. Catherine L. 2016. ATD Press. Alexandria, VA.

A Learn the Art of Avoiding Action for the Sake of Action. SmartBrief. June 23, 2017. Accessed July 15, 2017 at http://www.smart-brief.com/original/2017/06/learn-art-avoiding-action-sake-action-0?utm_source=brief.

Managing Your Mission-Critical Knowledge. Ihrig M., Macmillan I. *Harvard Business Review.* January–February 2015.

Mark Zuckerberg Supports Universal Basic Income. What is it? Gillespie P. May 26, 2017. CNN Money. Accessed September 27, 2017 at http://money.cnn.com/2017/05/26/news/economy/mark-zuckerberg-universal-basic-income/index.html

Marketing Management 12e. Kotler P., Keller K.L. 2006. Prentice-Hall of India. New Delhi.

The Monk Who Sold His Ferrari. Sharma R. 1997. HarperCollins. New York, NY.

Technology is Wiping Out Companies Faster Than Ever. Regalado A. *MIT Technology Review.* September 10, 2013. Accessed September 1, 2017 at https://www.technologyreview.com/s/519226/technology-is-wiping-out-companies-faster-than-ever/.

Teenage Team Develops AI to Screen for Diabetic Neuropathy. Jeff L. August 8, 2017. MobiHealthNews. Accessed August 8, 2017 at http://www.mobihealthnews.com/content/teenage-team-develops-ai-system-screen-diabetic-retinopathy.

Working with SMEs: A Guide to Gathering and Organizing Content from Subject Matter Experts. Salvatore P. 2018. Balboa Press. Bloomington, IN.

Resources

Here are some of the books, websites, software and people who contributed to this book either directly or by example and can provide you with related tools and information. Everything and everyone here is highly recommended.

The Science of Science Communication III: Inspiring Novel Collaborations and Building Capacity. A National Academy of Sciences conference November 16–17, 2017. Accessed September 27, 2017 at http://www.cvent.com/events/the-science-of-science-communication-iii-inspiring-novel-collaborations-and-building-capacity/ event-summary

On Mainframe Computing: Why the Mainframe Needs to Become More Mainstream. Chris Preimesberger. September 25, 2017. Accessed September 27, 2017 at http://www.eweek.com/pc-hardware/why-the-mainframe-needs-to-become-more-mainstream
Peter Diamandis website: Diamandis.com

Software

Knovio (KnowledgeVision) – WYSISYG software built for experts to collect video, audio, slides.
knovio.com
Synapse – Software built for experts to organize your training programs with the instructional design built in. Also excellent for instructional designers to build instructionally sound training.
getsynapse.com [use my personal link, TBD]

Books and Websites

Learning Environments by Design – Author Catherine Lombardozzi is one of the first authors to discuss the importance of microlearning and how it revolutionizes training approaches for a 24/7 learning audience.
L4LP.com
Peter Diamandis – Futurist Diamandis envisions the future and remains at the head of the pack of visionaries. Author of *Bold* and *Abundance*. Any book or podcast by Diamandis is well worth your time if you are in a position where you need to see around corners and lead yourself, others or your organization into the unknown. Diamandis will help you lead with wonder and imagination. His website is rich with links to his many projects and resources.
diamandis.com
Ray Kurzweil – Diamandis on steroids for nerds. Kurzweil wrote The Singularity is Near: When Humans Transcend Biology and The Age of Spiritual Machines: When Computers Exceed Human Intelligence. If you want to know how we get to the future, this is for you.
kurzweilai.net

Training for the Future

Karl Kapp – Author of *The Gamification of Learning and Instruction* and related books, Kapp also leads the Instructional Technology program at Bloomsburg University in Bloomsburg, PA. He is a professor, author, speaker and consultant out in front of the movement to make learning relevant using technology. If you are building learning programs for the 21st Century, check him out.

  karlkapp.com

Index

A

Accuracy, 186
Acknowledgement, of SME review, 181
ADDIE (Analysis, Design, Development, Implementation, and Evaluation) process, 24, 127–129, 132
  assigned SME and, 129–130
After Action Review, 183, 184
Age-related illnesses, and biological changes, 86–87
AI, *see* Artificial intelligence
Analysis phase, ADDIE model, 128, 130
Animal Farm (book), 192
Areste, Esther, 114
Artificial intelligence (AI), 101
  experts and, 195–199
Assets
  identifying critical, 52–53
  prioritizing and organizing, 51–52

Association for Talent Development (ATD), 77–78
ATD, *see* Association for Talent Development
Attitudes, 94–95
Audio capture of interview, 91
Austin, Ryan, 103
Automation, 21
Awareness, 121

B

Baby Boomers, 3, 27, 79–80, 99
Bad habits, avoiding, 28
Basic Control Account (BCA), 188
BCA, *see* Basic Control Account
Benford, Irvine Gregory, 104–105
Big picture thinking, 14–15
Biological changes, and age-related illnesses, 86–87
Biomedical research, 12
Bitcoin, 196
Blind spots, 187
Blumthal, Eric G., 103
Books, 92

Boomers, 85
Bradbury, Ray, 192
"Brilliant jerks" workshop, 119
Burch, Noel, 121
Bureau of Labor Statistics, 3, 4
Burke, Edmund, 125

C

Cassette, 18
Catch and release program, 44–45
C. F. Martin and Co., 109
Charts, 92
Childhood learning, 7–8
Coexistence, peaceful, 87
Common sense guidelines, for
        project managers, 173
Compaq™, 109
Competence, 121
Competitive advantages, 34
    capturing, 30–31
    chart, 71
    diagram, 35, 36–37, 39, 41, 51, 56
Conflicts, scheduling, 186
Confounding SMEs, 149–150
Conscious competent model, 121
Conscious incompetent model, 121
Content curation, 20, 106
    for deep learning, 9–10
    for shallow learning, 9
Content developers
    SME tear sheets for, 186–190
    tips/tricks/tools for, 162–184
        after action review template,
            184
        checklist for organizing
            information, 172
        common sense guidelines, 173
        content gathering session cover
            sheet, 176
        expert interview checklist, 178
        follow-up and wrap-up
            signoffs, 182

project charter checklist,
    168–171
project evaluation checklist,
    183
project plan checklist, 163–164
review cycle capture log,
    179–180
roles and responsibilities chart,
    174
SME acknowledgement of
    review, 181
SMEs contact list, 175
standard interview questions,
    177
working with Confounding
    SMEs, 149–150
working with Creative,
    Scattered SMEs, 140–141
working with Defensive
    SMEs, 144
working with Interrupted
    SMEs, 151–152
working with Not-Quite-
    Expert SMEs, 145–146
working with Overcommitted
    SMEs, 147–148
working with Reckless
    Reviewer, 153–154
working with Reluctant
    SMEs, 155–156
working with Shortcut SMEs,
    142
working with Speedy SME,
    139
writing project charter,
    165–167
working with experts, 133–135
Content gathering, 128, 190
cover sheet, 176
Content tags, 85
Continuous process improvement
    knowledge management
    flowchart, 23–24

Convolutional neural network, 199
Corporate assets
  capturing competitive
    advantages, 30
  completing competitive
    advantages diagram, 36–37
  examining organizational chart,
    25–28
  knowledge mapping, 33–36
  organizational forgetting, 28
  plan, 28–30
  prioritization of, 25–37
  value and distinction, 30–33
  value of exercise, 37
count5, 103
Critical assets
  essential information, 53
  non-essential information, 52–53
  value and distinction, 52–53
Critical information, 28–29
  focus on, 53–56
Critical knowledge, 5, 24, 26
Critical personnel loss, 58–59
Critical thinking, 107, 108
  teaching, 14–15
CRM, *see* Customer resource
    management
Cross-training initiative, 43
Cryptocurrency, 196, 197
Customer resource management
  (CRM), 69

D

Deadline problems, 173
Decision making, about value, 16
DEC, *see* Digital Equipment
    Corporation
Dedicated SMEs, 130–132, 157–159
Deep knowledge, 6–7, 13
  of future of the company, 16–19
Deep learning, 100
  content curation for, 9–10

*Deep Time: How Humanity
    Communicates Across
    Millenia* (book), 104
Defensive SMEs, 144
de Holan, Pablo Martin, 28
Demmitt, Dallas, 22–23
Demmitt, Nancy, 22–23
Design phase, ADDIE model, 128,
  130
Development phase, ADDIE
    model, 128, 130
Diagrams, 92
Diamandis, Peter H., 122–124
Digital Equipment Corporation
  (DEC), 62–63
Digital Gold (book), 196
Digital photography, 110
Disabilities, 86
Dreaming, 198
Dueling experts, 191

E

Early childhood learning, 7–8
Educational software, 92
Educational videos, 8
Elder advisors, team of, 82
Elder advocate, 82
E-learning programs, 94, 97
Electronic job aids, 8
Entitlement, 80
Entrepreneurship, 122
Essential information, 53
Evaluation, ongoing, 21–22
Evaluation phase, ADDIE model,
  128, 130
Exercises, value of, 37
Expert content contributor, process
  tips for, 186–187
Expertise, capturing
  collection/storage/delivery
    challenges for, 77–87
  creating tech plan for, 89–95

Experts
  artificial intelligence and, 195–199
  digression, 199–200
  dueling, 191
  of future, 191–200
  interview checklist, 178
  making plan to retaining human
    knowledge, 200
  managing, 122–126, 137–154,
    193–195
  societal application, 191–193
  tips for providing great
    information, 188–190
  traditional/nextgen, 193–195
Experts' discernment
  critical assets, identifying
    essential information, 53
    non-essential information,
      52–53
  finding knowledge and training
    gaps, 56
    checklist, 57–58
  focus on critical information,
    53–56
  4Ms methodology
    machine branch, 62–65
    man branch, 58–61
    materials branch, 65–69
    methods branch, 69–71
    prioritizing, 58–59
  knowledge stratification, 56–57
  prioritizing and organizing assets,
    51–52
  time and resource commitment,
    71–74
Extraneous information, 189

F

Fahrenheit 451 (book), 192
Failure to capture, 28
Family-owned businesses, 47–48
  succession planning for, 46

"Fire Your Experts!," 123, 125
Floppy disks, 18
Follow-up signoffs, 182
Ford, Henry, 123, 192
Founder's succession planning, 47
4Ms methodology, prioritizing
  machine branch, 62–65
  man branch, 58–61
  materials branch, 65–69
  methods branch, 69–71
Functional area exercise, 40–42,
  72, 91

G

Generational learning, transferring,
  78
Good introduction, 188
Google™, 99
Google Glass™, 99
Google X, 124
Greatest Generation, 3
Guild, 43

H

Hands-on practice, 95
Hard working, 82
Historical knowledge, 83
Historical preservation, 112–115
Hoffmeister, Mike, 100
Human expertise, 198
Human history, 191
Human judgment, obsolete of,
  198–199
Human knowledge, retaining, 200
Human resources, 173
Hutson, Steve, 197–198

I

IDs, *see* Instructional designers
Ihrig, Martin, 31–32

Implementation phase, ADDIE
    model, 128, 130
Inaccurate procedures, 189
Information
    checklist for organizing from
        SMEs, 172
    collecting, 8, 89–90
    storing and translating into
        learning materials, 92–93
Informed action, 15
In-house experts, 21
Innovation, 122
InnovationFail, 111–112
Instinctive knowledge, 55–56
Instructional designers (IDs), 97, 98,
    102, 127, 133, 173
Intergenerational challenges,
    affecting learning transfer,
    82–83
Internal experts, 17, 24, 129
International Space Station, 110
Internet, 11–12
Interrupted SMEs, 151–152
Interview
    expert checklist, 178
    standard questions, 177
Irreplaceable employee, 45–46
Irreplaceable knowledge, 73
Iteration, 15

J

James, William, 127
Journal articles, 92
Judgment calls, about value, 16
Just-in-time information, 8, 9–10

K

Keller, Kevin Lane, 31
Knovio®, 102
"Know-it-all-ness," 83
Knowledge, 94, 121

acquisition, 6
assets, 18–19
capturing, using experts,
    127–135
management, 25, 27–28, 51
mapping, 33
stratification, 56–57, 60, 63, 66,
    67, 72
Knowledge and training gap
    analysis, 72
    4Ms methodology, 60–61,
        63–64, 67–68, 70
    checklist, 57–58
    finding, 56
Knowledge, skills, and attitudes
    (KSAs), 4, 17, 23–24
KnowledgeVision®, 102
Kodak, 105, 110–111
    as poster child for
        #InnovationFail, 111–112
Kotler, Philip, 31
KSAs, *see* Knowledge, skills, and
    attitudes
Kurzweil, Ray, 21

L

Lagasse, Jeff, 199
Lawrence, Tracy, 28
Leadership, 29
    and influence, 59–60
Leadership Freak blog, 80–81
Learner's attitude, 82
Learning
    deep, 9–10
    early childhood, 7–8
    model, 121, 122
    needs, in age of industrial
        dislocation, 107–115
    shallow, 6–7
    to think like experts, 13–14
Learning Environments by Design
    (book), 11, 21

Learning transfer
  intergenerational challenges
    affecting, 82–83
  with multigenerational
    workforce, 79–80
Learn the Art of Avoiding Action for
    the Sake of Action (article), 15
Legacy learning management system
  (LMS), 98
Lists, 92
LMS, *see* Legacy learning
  management system
Lombardozzi, Catherine, 11, 21
Long-term planning, 15, 108

M

Machine branch, 37
  find gaps, 64–65
  knowledge and training gap
    exercise, 63–64
  prioritizing and organizing
    information, 63
  proprietary corporate computers,
    62–63
Macmillan, Ian, 31–32
Managing Your Mission-Critical
    Knowledge (article), 31–32
Man assets, 60
Man branch, 36, 58–61
  find gaps, 61
  knowledge and training gap
    exercise, 60–61
  leadership and influence, 59–60
  prioritizing and organizing assets,
    60
Manufacturing companies, 62
Marketing Management, 31
Maslow, Abraham, 121
Materials branch, 36–37
  common materials, 66
  knowledge and training gap
    exercise, 67–68

  prioritizing and organizing
    information, 66–67
  production of, 66
Measurement Engineering, 47
Medicare, 79
Meditation, 198
Me Generation, 79
Memory decay, 28
Methods branch, 37
  find your gaps, 71, 72
  knowledge and training gap
    exercise, 70
  prioritizing and organizing
    information, 70
  proprietary, 69–70
  replication of, 69
Milestones, scheduling, 173
Millennials, 77–78, 85
MobiHealthNews, 198
Model T Ford, 114
Multigenerational workforce,
    learning transfer with,
    79–80
Mutual respect and low threat
    interactions
  entitlement, 80
  for older gen, 80–81
  for younger gen, 81

N

National Academy of Sciences, 134
Neurolinguistic programming
  (NLP), 99–100
NextGen experts, 193–195
NLP, *see* Neurolinguistic
  programming
Non-essential information, 52–53,
  57–58, 85
Non-essential materials, 66
Notetaking, 91
Not-Quite-Expert SMEs, 145–146
Numbers, 17

O

Off-site meetings, 86
Older generation, 80–81
On-the-job training, 8
Organizational chart, 40–42
    examining, 25–28
Organizational forgetting, 28
Orwell, George, 192
OSHA compliance training, 53
Overcommitted SMEs, 147–148

P

Passions, and reasons, 191–193
Patent, 70
Peaceful coexistence, 87
People skills, 120
Perfect SMEs, 132–133, 137–138
Performance goals, 128
Period, 45
Personal interaction, 95
Philips, Nelson, 28
Pianesi, Adriano, 15
Plato, 183
Pokémon™, 109
Pokemon Go™, 99
Pontiac Firebird, 114
Poor introduction, 188
Popper, Nathaniel, 197
"Preinforcement," 103
Prietula, Michael J., 13
Project charter
    checklist, 168–171
    writing
        assessment and evaluation,
            166, 170
        assumptions, 166, 170
        audience, 166, 169
        about client, 165
        content, 165, 169
        deliverable requirements, 166,
            169

expected outcomes, 165, 169
project alerts, 167, 170
project goals, 165, 168
project management, 166, 170
project overview, 165, 168
project schedule, 166
project style guidelines, 167,
    171
purpose, 165
technical requirements, 166,
    169
upfront planning, 166
Project evaluation checklist, 183
Project managers
    tips/tricks/tools for, 162–184
        after action review template,
            184
        checklist for organizing
            information, 172
        common sense guidelines, 173
        content gathering session cover
            sheet, 176
        expert interview checklist,
            178
        follow-up and wrap-up
            signoffs, 182
        project charter checklist,
            168–171
        project evaluation checklist,
            183
        project plan checklist, 163–164
        review cycle capture log,
            179–180
        roles and responsibilities chart,
            174
        SME acknowledgement of
            review, 181
        SMEs contact list, 175
        standard interview questions,
            177
        writing project charter,
            165–167
Project plan checklist, 163–164

Proprietary corporate computers, 62–63
Pull learning, 11
Push learning, 11

Q

Q.MINDshare™, 103
Quality improvement, 18

R

Rapid response iteration, 15
Reagan, Ronald, 10
Real learning, 101
Reckless Reviewer SMEs, 153–154
Recording tape, 18
Recycling, 20
Rehirement, 44–45
Relevance, 20
Reluctant SMEs, 42–44, 155–156
Repetition, 6
Resource allocation, for knowledge capture, 112
Resource commitment, 71–74
Respect, 82
Restricted web access, 12
Retirement and rehirement, 44–45
Retiring experts, 193
Revenue generating asset, 113
Review cycle capture log, 179–180
Review cycles, 21–22
Robots, 196, 200
Rockwell, Dan, 80, 81–82
Roles and responsibilities chart, 174
Root cause analysis diagram, 35–36

S

Schedule updates, 173
Scheduling conflicts, 186
Seasoned experts, blending, 125
Second Life™, 100

7 Ways Young Leaders Succeed with Elders (Leadership Freak blog), 81–82
Shallow knowledge, 14
Shallow learning, 6–7
content curation for, 9
Sharma, Robin, 119
Shelf life, 98
Shelfware, 19
Shortcuts, 189
Signoffs, 187
Simon, Herbert A., 13
Singularity University, 123
Siri™, 99
Skills, 94–95
Skype, 78
Slide presentations, 91
Smartphones, 8, 77
SMEs, *see* Subject matter experts
"Snag, tag, and bag" expert, 120
Social Security, 79
Soft skills, 120
Software, 98
Speeches, 91
Speedy SMEs, 139
Strategic planning, 7
Strategic thinking, 15
Stratification exercises, 107
Subject matter experts (SMEs), 16, 26, 73, 90
acknowledgement of review, 181
and ADDIE process, 129–130
catch and release program, 44–45
Confounding, 149–150
considerations for working with, 132–133
contact list, 175
Creative, Scattered, 140–141
dedicated, 130–132, 157–159
Defensive, 144
four stages of learning model, 121, 122
for Hire, 157–159

identifying by functional area and role, 41, 42
Interrupted, 151–152
managing experts, 122–126
nature of, 119–126
Not-Quite-Expert, 145–146
Overcommitted, 147–148
Perfect, 138
Reckless Reviewer, 153–154
Reluctant, 42–44, 155–156
Shortcut, 142–143
Speedy, 138–139
succession planning with, 39–49
tips/tricks/tools for, 185–190
trouble with, 120–121
working with, 5–6, 120
Succession planning, 25, 27
for family-owned businesses, 46
founder, 47
with SMEs, 39–49
Super 8 camera, 105, 111
Synapse®, 103

T

Tear sheets
for content developer, 186–190
SME, 134–135
Technological comfort zone, 83–86
Technology changes, 98–99
Teenage Team Develops AI to Screen for Diabetic Neuropathy, 199
Teleportation, 110
Teller, Astro, 124
Templates, toolkit of, 173
Terminal objectives, 128
"Think outside the box," 111
30 Days to the New Economy (ebook), 107
3D printing, 110, 111
Time and resource commitment, 71–74
Timeliness, 186

Traditional experts, 194–195
Training
experts, 84
unnecessary programs, 20
as world's oldest profession, 7–9

U

UBI, *see* Universal Basic Income
Unconscious competent model, 121
Unconscious incompetent model, 121
Undiffused information, 32, 33
Union, 43
Universal Basic Income (UBI), 197
Unlearning, 28
Unstructured information, 32, 33
User-friendly knowledge capture tools, 97

V

Value adding, 82
Value and distinction, 30–36
Value of exercises, 37
Video capture of interview, 91
Vinyl audio records, 105
Virtual reality (VR), 99–100
VR, *see* Virtual reality
VUCA (volatile, uncertain, complex, and ambiguous) world, 15

W

Web access, 11–12
Webinars, 94
What-you-see-is-what-you-get (WYSIWYG) simplicity, 83
White papers, 92
Workforce, 3, 4
Workplaces, 27
World War II generation, 3

Wrap-up signoffs, 182
WYSIWYG simplicity, *see* What-
    you-see-is-what-you-get
    (WYSIWYG) simplicity

X

XPrize, 123

Y

Younger generation, 81
"You've-gotta-do-it-to-get-it," 100
Zuckerberg, Mark, 197